THE
THRIFTY GUIDE TO THE
AMERICAN REVOLUTION
A HANDBOOK FOR TIME TRAVELERS

THE
THRIFTY GUIDE TO THE
AMERICAN REVOLUTION
A HANDBOOK FOR TIME TRAVELERS

JOIN, or DIE.

Jonathan W. Stokes
illustrated by David Sossella

VIKING

VIKING
Penguin Young Readers
An imprint of Penguin Random House LLC
375 Hudson Street
New York, New York 10014

First published in the United States of America by Viking,
an imprint of Penguin Random House LLC, 2018

LIBRARY OF CONGRESS CATALOGING-IN-PUBLICATION DATA IS AVAILABLE
ISBN 9781101998113 (hardcover)
ISBN 9780451479617 (paper-over-board)

Manufactured in China
Book design, graphs, and maps by Mariam Quraishi

1   3   5   7   9   10   8   6   4   2

For Zach Greenberger

PREFACE

The Thrifty Guide to the American Revolution was published holographically by Time Corp in the year 2164. It offers a complete vacation package for tourists visiting the American Revolution. A careless time traveler accidentally lost a copy of this handy guidebook in our own era, along with guides to Ancient Rome, Ancient Greece, and even the Middle Ages. A New York publishing house decided to republish these books without the permission of Time Corp, since attempts to contact the future have been unsuccessful.

The Thrifty Guide to the American Revolution provides useful information for the practical time traveler:

- Where can I find a decent hotel room in colonial New England? Are credit cards accepted?

- How can I join the Boston Tea Party without winding up in a British prison?

- What do I do if I'm being shot at by a cannon?

This guide answers these fiery, burning questions with the marshmallows of information. There is handy advice on how to join Paul Revere's spy ring at the Green Dragon Tavern, how to enlist in General Washington's rebel army, and how to summon the strength to storm a British gun battery when you haven't eaten for three days. So pick up your fife and powder your ponytail. What follows is the original *Thrifty Guide to the American Revolution,* as it was discovered on a sidewalk outside Frank's Pizza in Manhattan in AD 2018....

THE THRIFTY GUIDE TO THE AMERICAN REVOLUTION

A HANDBOOK FOR TIME TRAVELERS

TIME CORP!™ SERVING YESTERDAY, FOR A BETTER TOMORROW, TODAY.™

INTRODUCTION BY TIME CORP'S
CORPORATE OVERLORD,
FINN GREENQUILL

The Thrifty Guide to the American Revolution is a thrilling vacation package for anyone interested in US history, or for cheapskate time travelers too stingy to buy our vacation package to the Renaissance. Let's be honest, winning independence from the British Empire is no picnic. If you find yourself starving with George Washington's troops at Valley Forge, eating tree bark, and cutting off your own frostbitten toes, don't say we didn't warn you.[*]

The Thrifty Guides are the best guidebooks in all of history. We know because we've checked. They contain the whole scope of human knowledge. If it's not in these

---

[*] You are welcome to call our complaint line at 1-999-WHINERS, but the number is out of order. For complaints about our complaint line, you can call our complaint line complaint line at 1-999-TUFFLUK. This line doesn't work either.

guidebooks, it didn't happen. This book is known to cure several illnesses, including measles, dengue fever, and cornpuff syndrome.[*]

We encourage you to buy a Time Corp life insurance policy before joining the Revolutionary army. If you are shot by a British musket, just remember, you signed a waiver. Enjoy your trip to the American Revolution!

Signed,

Finn Greenquill

Finn Greenquill
Founder and Corporate Overlord, Time Corp

....

* Time Corp's lawyers wish to make clear they were not consulted in the writing of these grandiose statements. Also, cornpuff syndrome is not even a disease.

FOREWORD

Time Corp is a company with heart. We care about supporting worthy causes. A portion of the proceeds of this book will be donated to the following charities:

$ Help Find a Cure for Finn Greenquill's Lack of Fabergé Eggs

$ Make a Wish for Finn Greenquill to Have More Fabergé Eggs

$ Help Orphaned Fabergé Eggs Find a Home in Finn Greenquill's Collection

$ The Society for the Expansion of Finn Greenquill's Bubble Gum Ball

$ The Foundation for Blowing Up the Moon on Finn's Birthday

$ The Finn Greenquill Legal Defense Fund

$ The Finn Greenquill Endangered Panda Catapult

TIME CORP LIMITATION OF LIABILITY

By reading this Thrifty Guide, you agree to and accept the following:

1. Time paradoxes and world conflicts caused during time travel must be resolved at the time traveler's own expense.

2. Time travelers killed by the British Army will receive no refund for this book.

3. Billions made in the stock market are yours to enjoy. However, under no circumstances may you transport ancient fruits and vegetables across temporal lines.

4. Time travelers visiting the past to give away TV spoilers will have their past-ports revoked unconditionally.

5. Whoever cracked the Liberty Bell, we will find you eventually.

6. George Washington is tired of being everyone's lunch date. He asks that you respect his social calendar. Former US president Millard Fillmore, however, wishes to announce that he is very much available.

7. Transporting saber-toothed tigers to the Battle of Bunker Hill is hilarious, but illegal.

Time Corp Worldwide Headquarters in New New New New New New New York, AD 2164

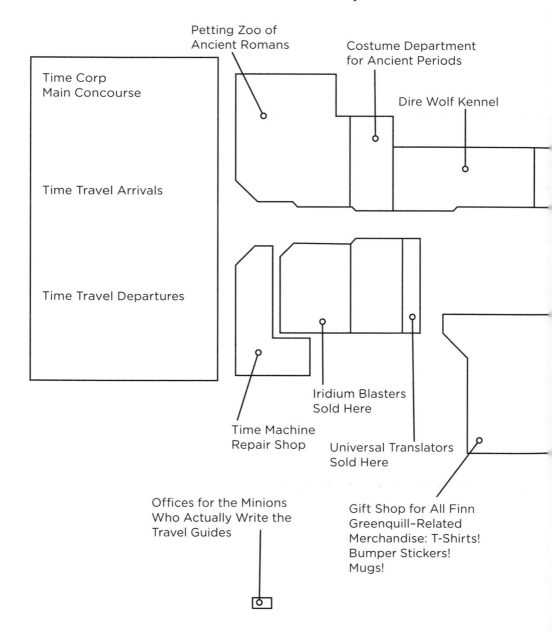

Petting Zoo of Ancient Romans

Costume Department for Ancient Periods

Dire Wolf Kennel

Time Corp Main Concourse

Time Travel Arrivals

Time Travel Departures

Iridium Blasters Sold Here

Time Machine Repair Shop

Universal Translators Sold Here

Offices for the Minions Who Actually Write the Travel Guides

Gift Shop for All Finn Greenquill–Related Merchandise: T-Shirts! Bumper Stickers! Mugs!

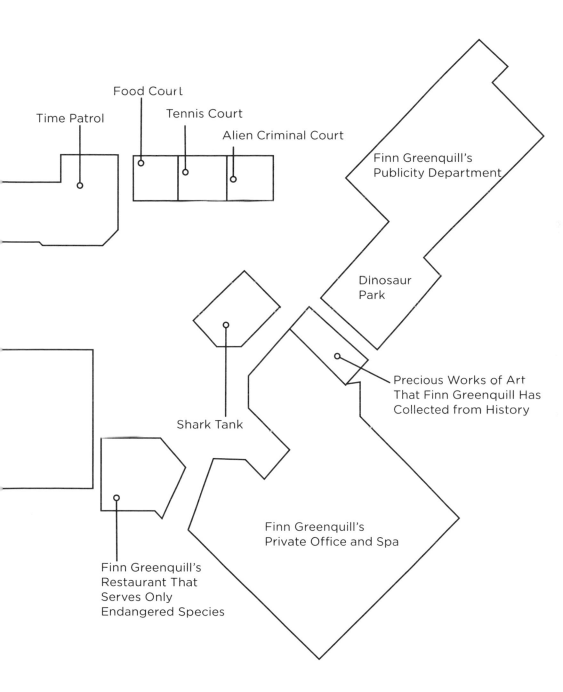

Time Patrol

Food Court

Tennis Court

Alien Criminal Court

Finn Greenquill's
Publicity Department

Dinosaur
Park

Precious Works of Art
That Finn Greenquill Has
Collected from History

Shark Tank

Finn Greenquill's
Private Office and Spa

Finn Greenquill's
Restaurant That
Serves Only
Endangered Species

CONTENTS

INTRODUCTION
THE BASICS OF TIME TRAVEL

1. Intro to Time Travel

On the first day of physics class, when freeze-rays are handed out, everyone asks their physics professor what happens if you go back in time and freeze yourself before you go back in time to freeze yourself. The answer is so maddening, many students go back in time to freeze their physics professors. Or, occasionally, to simply register for a different class.

No one has yet studied what would happen if physics professors were sent back in time to freeze themselves before they became physics professors. Though, it should be noted, several physics professors have been known to go back in time to freeze other physics professors.

It would stand to reason that the laws of physics would apply to physics professors, even though physics professors are technically the ones defining the laws of physics. It's possible that if physics professors weren't happy with the laws of physics, they could simply invent some new laws of physics, and the rest of us would be none the wiser. It's not as though anyone but a physics professor would be nutty enough to go around questioning the laws of physics.

It is unlikely any physics professors would go back in time to freeze themselves before they had made tenure. However, tenured physics professors could probably go back in time to freeze themselves quite safely, because as any university can tell you, it's nearly impossible to get rid of a tenured professor.

2. The Rules of Time Travel

The First Rule of Time Travel is that no one is allowed to permanently change the past except Finn Greenquill. Got a problem with that? Hey, if you want to permanently alter human history, *you* invent time travel.[*]

Finn's ability to do whatever he wants with history enables several very important causes:

- Supplying Finn's four-star restaurant that serves only endangered species

- Beefing up Finn's eighteenth-century art collection. The one he plans on selling in the twenty-third century for an astronomical profit

- Collecting prehistoric fish to feed the sixty-foot megalodon shark in Finn's office aquarium

....

[*] The writers of this time travel guide wish the reader to know that we did not write this section. Finn wrote all of it. Or rather, he dictated it from his bubble bath while forcing us to take notes.

Finn also takes credit for causing Napoleon's stunning defeat at Waterloo, America landing a man on the moon, and the inexplicable popularity of electronic dance music in the twenty-first century. But these claims are extremely difficult to prove.

HELPFUL HINTS:
SIGNS YOU ARE CAUGHT IN A TIME LOOP

- If this section sounds familiar, as if you've read it millions of times, you may be caught in a time loop.

- If you have déjà vu of having déjà vu, you may be caught in a time loop.

- If your day planner for tomorrow resembles everything you did yesterday, you may be caught in a time loop.

- If you check your credit card statement and realize you've purchased this book eight thousand times, thank you. But also, you may be caught in a time loop.

- If you have déjà vu of having déjà vu, you may be caught in a time loop.

3. Time Patrol

The good people at the Time Patrol do an excellent job of cleaning up history after you are done time traveling. If you accidentally borrow Paul Revere's horse, preventing him from making his famous ride, the Time Patrol will return Paul's horse before you borrow it, fixing your changes to history.

Sometimes the Time Patrol makes mistakes. After all, they are only human. Luckily, we have the Time Patrol Time Patrol, who do an excellent job of cleaning up any mistakes made by the Time Patrol. Of course, the Time Patrol Time Patrol are only human. Which is why we have the Time Patrol Time Patrol Time Patrol, who do an excellent job of cleaning up mistakes made by the Time Patrol Time Patrol.

Mistakes made by the Time Patrol Time Patrol Time Patrol are cleaned up by the Time Patrol. Who are, of course, policed by the Time Patrol Time Patrol.

4. Your Time Machine

What better way to cruise around colonial America than in your very own one-horse carriage? The Time Corp Time Machine Colonial™ features reclining seats, cup holders, and a convenient weapons rack for holding muskets, rifles, and iridium blasters. The state-of-the-art cloaking device will allow you to slip past

British sentries unobserved. And Time Corp offers free roadside assistance for up to ten thousand years. So what are you waiting for? Grab your musket and hop in your time machine—it's time to join the American Revolution!

Your Time Corp Time Machine Colonial ™

Storage for spare iridium blasters and portable Time Corp Time Travel Devices™

Antennae for better phone reception when communicating with the future

People not included with purchase

Bionically enhanced horses reach speeds of up to two hundred mph

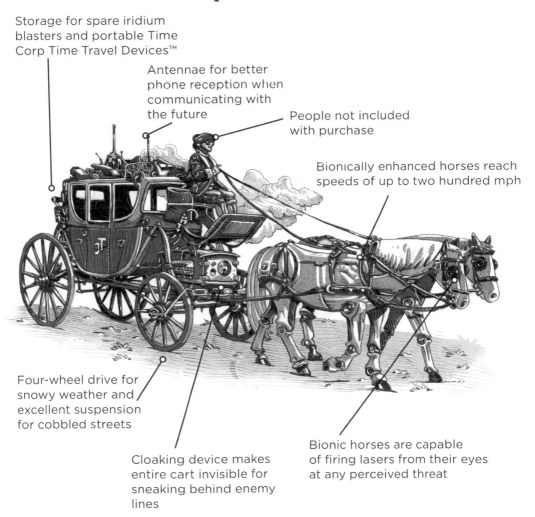

Four-wheel drive for snowy weather and excellent suspension for cobbled streets

Cloaking device makes entire cart invisible for sneaking behind enemy lines

Bionic horses are capable of firing lasers from their eyes at any perceived threat

1

THE BOSTON TEA PARTY

Generally, Finn Greenquill isn't a fan of revolutions or democracy, because these sorts of things tend to make his employees get riled up and start asking for health benefits and paid vacation days. Nevertheless, the American Revolution is one of Time Corp's most popular—*and* profitable—time traveling vacations, as well as one of the most unlikely David and Goliath stories in all of history.

Set your time machine for 1773. The seventeen-year-old musical genius Mozart is stunning audiences on his tour through Italy. Captain James Cook is becoming the first European explorer to cross the Antarctic Circle. And in America, a ragtag band of untrained rebels is about to go to war against the most powerful army in the world.

Welcome to Massachusetts

Your trip begins in the colony of Massachusetts. Like all the thirteen colonies in America, Massachusetts is under British rule. The first colonists land on Plymouth Rock in 1620. Freezing, starving, and unable to grow food, half the original settlers die in the first winter.*

You may be wondering what sort of crazy Englishmen actually choose to live in Massachusetts in the 1600s. Let's face it: leaving Mother England to cross the three-thousand-mile-wide Atlantic Ocean is sort of like moving to Mars. A settler is never going to see their home, their friends, and their family ever again. And for what? To live in a cold, rocky, mosquito-infested land filled with the constant threat of war, disease, starvation, and lousy baseball teams.

There is a reason many settlers choose to make this dangerous journey: a little something called freedom. In England at this time, everyone must practice one religion, called "the Church of England." If you miss church on Sunday, you are fined. And if you practice a different religion, you can be imprisoned or even executed.

The settlers choose to live three thousand miles from England so they can be three thousand miles from England's laws and three thousand miles from England's king. Many of them come from small religious groups like the Puritans or the Quakers. They sail to America to find the freedom to practice their religions.† Other settlers move to America for a better chance of finding land and wealth. What all the American colonists have in common is a strong independent streak—they don't like to be bossed around by the English king.

....

* If you time travel to the Plymouth settlement, bring lots of snacks and some vitamin C.

† Note: Not everyone in America has religious freedom yet. For instance, if you are Catholic and try to visit the colony of Massachusetts, you will be thrown in prison.

Welcome to Boston

It's now 153 years after the colonists' arrival at Plymouth Rock, and Massachusetts has swelled to support a thriving population. The city of Boston is a bustling seaport with over fifteen thousand citizens. Hundreds of buildings line the cobbled streets, and dozens of European and Caribbean ships fill the harbor.

Massachusetts is ruled by King George III of England. Not only is he three thousand miles away, but he is only thirty-five years old, and—oh, yeah—he suffers from occasional bouts of insanity. He's never attended a university and never set foot in America. And yet this is the guy in charge of running the American colonies.

THIRTEEN
COLONIES & BRITAIN

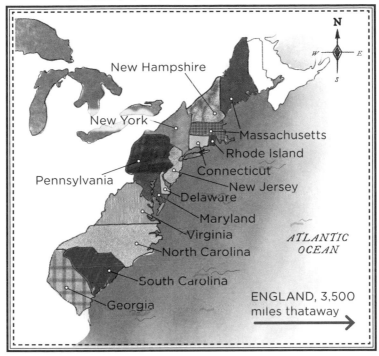

This isn't even that weird. In 1773, virtually every country in the world is ruled by a king or queen. No country can vote for their own leader. No country truly guarantees the right to freedom of speech, freedom of religion, or freedom of press. These basic rights simply don't exist in the world in 1773.* The people of Boston, and of all the colonies, have almost no say in the laws passed by the British government and in the taxes they have to pay to the king.

This means that if Britain passes an unfair law, there isn't a whole lot the Americans can do about it. If the thirteen fledgling

---

* These basic freedoms still don't exist in many parts of the world today (certainly not at Time Corp).

American colonies want to form their own government, they're going to have an uphill battle ahead of them. If the Americans rebel against the British king and demand independence from Britain, they will find themselves fighting the largest army, the largest navy, and the largest empire on the planet.

The Boston Tea Party

Your time travel adventure begins in Boston, Massachusetts, on the night of December 16, 1773. More than five thousand angry citizens—a third of the city's population—gather at the Old South Meeting House. Merchants, sailors, lawyers, farmers, and tradesmen overflow the meeting house and crowd the cobbled streets. They are hopping mad over two of the most important things in life: tea* and money.†

Stand in the back of the meeting house, where you won't get trampled by the furious crowd. Samuel Adams, the American politician who called the meeting, tries to keep order. The British government is forcing the Americans to buy all their tea from only a few British tea merchants . . . and two of the tea merchants just happen to be the British governor's own sons. These shenanigans will put a lot of American merchants out of business.

Adding insult to injury, the British are forcing Americans to pay a tea tax. The Americans are not allowed a vote over any

---

* Tea is important to the settlers because they are mostly descendants of the British, and tea is more or less sacred to British people.

† Money is important to the settlers because you need it to buy more tea.

of this. It's as if the British are robbing the Americans, and then forcing them to pay a robbery tax.

When the British refuse to back down on the tea tax, Samuel Adams tells the rowdy audience, "This meeting can do nothing more to save the country!" Samuel believes the tax is unfair and the Americans should rebel against the British to make their point.

See if you can spot John Hancock in the crowd. He's a wealthy Harvard graduate who will go on to become the first signer of the Declaration of Independence. John made his fortune selling Dutch tea. The new law forcing Americans to buy only British tea will force him out of business. Watch as he stands up in the meeting house and shouts to the riotous crowd, "Let every man do what is right in his own eyes!"

That night, about one hundred American rebels set out to destroy all the British tea in Boston Harbor. The Americans would

rather have no tea than British tea. They dress up as Mohawk Indians, darkening their faces with soot to mask their identities from any witnesses. Two thousand Bostonians cheer from the docks of Griffin's Wharf. Find a good disguise and join the rebels as they ransack all three British tea ships. Together, you'll smash open 342 chests of tea with tomahawks, hurl the tea into Boston Harbor, and launch the American rebellion.

THINGS THE BOSTONIANS ARE MAD ABOUT

1. The Sugar Act (unfair taxes)

2. The Stamp Act (unfair taxes)

3. The Townshend Act (unfair taxes)

4. The Tea Act (unfair taxes)

5. The Boston Massacre (Bostonians shot by British soldiers for rioting against unfair taxes)

OTHER THINGS THE BOSTONIANS SHOULD BE MAD ABOUT

1. Hamburgers won't be invented for another hundred years

2. Boston won't have reliable Internet service for another 240 years

3. The Boston Red Sox will only win the World Series eight times in the next two centuries

HOW TO DRESS IN COLONIAL AMERICA

Understanding ancient fashions is very tricky, and time travelers often have enormous trouble blending in to colonial America. Instead of wearing a powdered wig on their head, they'll accidentally wear a powdered doughnut. Or instead of wearing a tricorne hat, they'll wear a candy corn hat. Or some time travelers will forget to use their horse for travel, and simply fire up their jetpack.* Any of these innocent

---

* Jetpacks do not get invented until 2121 and are not made illegal until the great Black Friday collision of 2126 that injures seven hundred shoppers as they jetpack simultaneously into a single shopping mall entrance in Poughkeepsie, New York.

mistakes will completely blow your cover in 1773.

Here are some fashion tips for blending in to Colonial Boston:

MEN

WOMEN

Tricorne hat

Powdered wig

Cap

Waistcoat

Frock coat

Dress supported by stays (a bodice with strips of whalebone) and hooped petticoats

Fashionable women carry folding fans.

Breeches

Gown

Stockings

Petticoat

Buckled shoes

Note: Women in the 1700s do not wear underpants.

The Intolerable Acts

Paul Revere is a silversmith who secretly helps organize the Boston Tea Party. Afterward, he rides his horse two hundred miles, all the way to New York City, to spread word about the revolt. The New Yorkers then join the rebellion and host their own tea party, dumping tea chests into the New York harbor. More rebellions soon spread throughout the thirteen colonies.

The British government is infuriated. There is no greater way to offend an Englishman than to destroy perfectly good tea. One member of the British government, Charles Van,[*] declares that Boston should be wiped off the face of the earth—destroyed like the ancient city of Carthage. King George III agrees to crack down on the rebels with an iron fist. He enacts a set of laws to punish Boston—they're the ones who started this mess.

The Bostonians find these acts so intolerable that they call them, well, the Intolerable Acts. British general Thomas Gage takes over Boston, flooding the streets with red-coated soldiers.[†] Gage's army commandeers American houses for troops and barns for horses. The British soldiers shut down Boston Harbor. They outlaw the local government and make it illegal to sue British officials in court. Then, to rub salt in the wound, the British give part of Massachusetts to its Canadian colony.

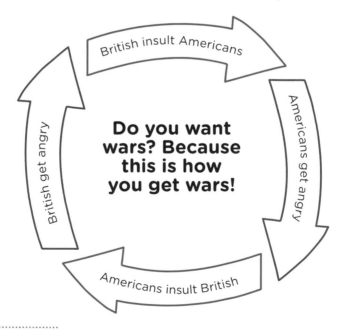

British insult Americans

Americans get angry

Do you want wars? Because this is how you get wars!

British get angry

Americans insult British

....

* No relation to Charles Car, Charles Bus, Charley Train, or Chuck Dirigible.

† Often called "redcoats," possibly owing to their red coats, though this is only a theory.

The Sons of Liberty

The American rebels form secret groups throughout the colonies called the Sons of Liberty. The Boston Sons of Liberty meet at the Green Dragon Tavern on Union Street in the North End. Many of the Founding Fathers of America are here, plotting a revolution to overthrow British rule. Sneak inside to attend a meeting.

The Sons of Liberty run a spy ring tracking British troop movements. These thirty Boston spies include Paul Revere, Samuel Adams, and John Hancock, as well as future American general Henry Knox. If you look around the candlelit room, you'll see future signers of the Declaration of Independence. And you'll also see the leader of all the rebels in Massachusetts, Dr. Joseph Warren.

Always be careful when dealing with spies—there may be double agents. Harvard graduate Benjamin Church, a member of the Sons of Liberty, is actually a British spy. He sells information to the British because he is deeply in debt and needs the money.

Benedict Arnold, who also meets at the Green Dragon, will eventually turn traitor and fight for the British. Remember, nearly everyone has British accents in colonial America, so there's no way to tell an American from a Brit. There's certainly no way to tell if a person is loyal to the British king or to the American rebels. Just keep an eye on Benjamin Church, and don't lend him any money.

Food: ★★
Noise Level: Hushed whispers 👏
Decor: ★
Wheelchair Accessible: No ✖
Service: ★★★
Accepts Credit Cards: No ✖
Cost: $ $ $
Attire: Cloak and dagger

The Green Dragon is also a meeting place for a secret club called the Freemasons. John Hancock and Paul Revere are both Freemasons, as well as Founding Fathers like Benjamin Franklin and George Washington. The Freemasons communicate using secret symbols and handshakes. Little is known about the origins of this ancient fraternity, but the Freemasons still exist today—many US presidents, senators, and even astronauts are members of this secret order.[*]

[*] Finn Greenquill is not a member of the Freemasons. But if anyone can let him into a secret meeting, he will greatly appreciate it. Finn makes a mean onion dip and promises he will pay his membership dues promptly.

With all the attention on secret meetings, it's amazing the staff of the Green Dragon has any time to actually cook food. But you'll be pleasantly surprised by the fare. Cider, coffee, and even hot chocolate are popular. The first chocolate factory in America opens in 1765 in Massachusetts. Good news—ice cream is also popular in colonial America.

Colonists grow onions, turnips, parsnips, and carrots, all of which make for a great stew. The food is bland but the rates are reasonable. Do yourself a favor and try the venison. Just don't order tea—the rebels will throw you in Boston Harbor.

Here is what some of our readers say about the Green Dragon Tavern:

★★ "I'm allergic to hay. I asked for allergy-free, dust-mite-proof, synthetic pillows, and clean sheets with a thread count of at least four hundred. The tavern management took my money and made me sleep in the stable."

—Dorothy S., Westport, CT

★★★★ "The Green Dragon Tavern is an excellent place to gather information from the rebels. What? Oh, I meant to say food—it's an excellent place to gather food from the rebels, who are the most wonderful cooks. And companions. Because I'm on their side, all the way. And I'm not a British spy. Um, I have to go now. Go, rebels!"

—Benjamin Church, not a spy for the British

★ "When I popped into the tavern for a drink, everyone fell silent. No one wanted to talk with me. I stayed a full hour and nobody uttered a single peep. Not a very friendly establishment."

—A British redcoat

The Road to War

The more the British punish Boston, the more the thirteen colonies band together. All the colonies except Georgia decide to form a Continental Congress. That means that, for the first time, representatives from each colony on the continent meet together to form an alliance. They all agree to boycott buying British goods. One by one, the colonies start building armies in case the British attack. On March 23, 1775, you can visit Richmond, Virginia, to see the great orator Patrick Henry give his famous speech—"Give me liberty or give me death!" His speech convinces the Virginia colony to prepare for battle with Britain. Two men in the audience will soon become very important to the rebel cause: Thomas Jefferson and George Washington.

The Americans have had enough of British tyranny. They want freedom. The colonies agree that any attack the British make on Massachusetts will be an attack on all the colonies. No longer a collection of independent provinces, the colonies are forming one country, united against the British. And the lines are drawn for war. . . .

2

THE BATTLES OF LEXINGTON AND CONCORD

Set your Time Corp Time Machine Colonial™ to April 18, 1775, and get some rest, because you are not going to have another chance to sleep for the next twenty-four hours. The good news is, things are about to get very exciting. The bad news is, well, you're probably going to get shot by a British musket.*

British general Thomas Gage controls Boston with 4,500 troops. Think about that—that's like one hundred NFL football teams, except with guns. Put another way, there is one British soldier for every three Bostonians. The people of Boston are kept under curfew—unable to leave their houses at night. When they feel like it, the British soldiers kick people out of their houses, eat their food, and sleep in their beds.

Meanwhile, the colonists in each Massachusetts town are training their own feeble volunteer militias to try to resist the massive British Army. Fat chance! Each measly American town

....
* Sorry, there are no refunds on Time Corp time travel vacations.

militia is made up of any locals who want to join. This includes wrinkled old men or skinny young boys, and none have professional military training.

The Americans need weapons and ammunition if they want to rebel against the British. When the British government learns the rebels are stockpiling ammunition in the Boston suburb of Concord, they order General Gage to march seven hundred redcoats out there to capture the supply and squelch the rebellion. While he's at it, Gage is ordered to arrest Samuel Adams and John Hancock, two of the leaders of the rebellion, who are hiding out in the nearby town of Lexington.

Unfortunately for Gage, the rebel spy group the Sons of Liberty discovers Gage's secret orders before he even receives them. . . .

The Midnight Ride of Paul Revere

The Sons of Liberty know the British redcoats plan to march to Concord at night, but they don't know which night, and they don't know whether the British will leave Boston by land or by crossing the Charles River. Because they don't have cell phones, the Sons of Liberty set up a secret code: "One if by land, two if by sea." If their spies see the British soldiers march by land, they'll shine one lantern in the belfry of the Old North Church. If the British row across the Charles River into Cambridge, the spies will shine two lanterns.*

---

* Why the Sons of Liberty call the Charles River "the sea" is a question you'll have to ask them. We don't know the answer.

COLONIAL BOSTON

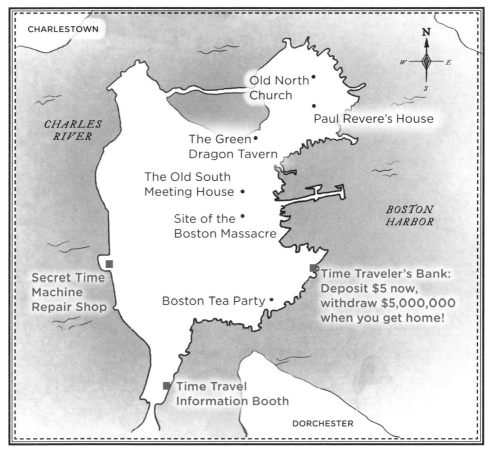

On the night of April 18, the British Army makes its move: they begin crossing the Charles River. The rebel spies send their signal: two lanterns shine from the steeple of the Old North Church. One of the best rebel riders—Paul Revere—sneaks across the river in a rowboat. On the other side, rebels provide him with a horse. You can ride with him tonight, but try to keep a low profile. Remember, Boston is under military curfew, so no one is allowed to leave their houses after dark. Paul Revere spurs his horse to a gallop and takes off on his midnight ride.

PRANKING THE PAST

If you want to help Paul Revere spread the word that the British are coming, try upgrading his horse to a motorcycle. Something fast and sporty, yet sensibly priced, like a Kawasaki Ninja with digital fuel injection and a 649cc four-stroke engine.

Or, if you really want to help Paul Revere spread the word faster, get him a cell phone.

BRITISH REDCOAT

AMERICAN REBEL

Bayonet

Red uniform

Musket

No uniform

No bayonet

Musket or rifle

Little or no professional training or military experience

Age 18-35

Age 14-75

Revere first gallops to the town of Lexington, warning every house along the way that the redcoats are coming. Local militiamen grab their guns, change out of their nightgowns, and gather on the town green. Revere warns John Hancock and Samuel Adams that they need to escape Lexington before the British arrest them. Rebel riders, devoted to the American cause, hear Revere's warnings and gallop on to warn Concord. There, more riders are alerted. By daybreak, the word spreads as far north as New Hampshire and as far south as Connecticut. American patriots grab their muskets and race to defend Concord from the British.

THE MIDNIGHT RIDE
of PAUL REVERE

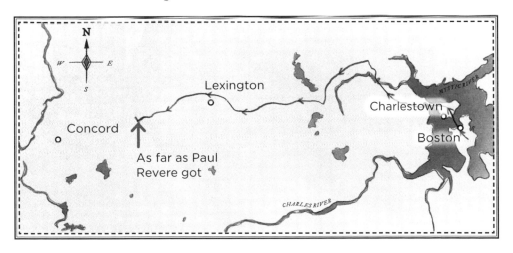

Meanwhile, seven hundred British redcoats board deep-bottomed boats to cross the Charles River out of Boston. Because of the bulky size of the boats, the soldiers must wade through waist-deep water to reach the shore. At two in the morning, wet and laden with equipment, they commence their seventeen-mile march to Concord. Their first stop, however, is in the town of Lexington to arrest Adams and Hancock. But by the time they set foot on the Lexington town green, they find a group of rebel militia waiting to greet them.

The Battle of Lexington—The Shot Heard 'Round the World

The British redcoats reach Lexington at sunrise on April 19, 1775. The Lexington militia—about eighty men—stand in ranks on the village common. It is just a show of force. The eighty men know they cannot stop seven hundred British troops.

You can join the fifty-odd spectators lining the roadside. Or, if you're feeling plucky, you can join the Lexington militia. Captain John Parker has tuberculosis and can't take deep breaths, so his voice is hard to hear. He orders his rebels, "Stand your ground. Don't fire unless fired upon."

But wouldn't you know it . . . somebody fires their gun.

No time traveler has ever been able to figure out whether it is a Brit or an American who fires the first shot.* Either way, once the shot rings out, the British soldiers break ranks and charge without orders. Within seconds, the redcoats slaughter eight of

....
* Finn Greenquill insists it was not him. He didn't fire the shot. Why would you even think that? The accusation is preposterous! He has no further comment at this time.

the Lexington militia and wound ten more. The outnumbered American rebels flee into the woods.

HELPFUL HINTS:
HOW TO FIRE A MUSKET

This is the end the bullet comes out of.

So you're being fired on by British redcoats. It happens to the best of us. This might be a good time to learn how to fire your musket. Just follow these easy steps:

1. Tear open a cartridge of powder charge with your teeth. **NOTE:** It will taste of salt and dry out your mouth. By the end of a battle, you'll be incredibly thirsty.

2. Drop a lead musket ball into the muzzle of your gun.

3. Check on the charging enemy troops. Are you dead yet? If not, proceed to step 4.

4. Shove the musket ball deep into your gun barrel using a ramrod. **NOTE:** Remember to remove the ramrod—don't fire it at the enemy.

5. If you're having trouble loading your musket, it's best to keep the muzzle clean with warm water. In a pinch, rebel soldiers actually use urine to get the job done.

6. Quick check—are you dead yet? No? Stop peeing and proceed to step 7.

7. Pour gunpowder into the firing pan. **NOTE**: Always keep the firing pan dry. If it gets wet from rain, it won't fire, and you will probably be bayoneted* to death by the British.

8. Quick check—still not dead? Proceed to step 9.

9. Pull back the hammer to cock the weapon. Raise the musket to your shoulder. The weapon weighs about ten pounds, so remember to hit the gym if you want steady aim. **NOTE**: Always aim low. Rookie soldiers often fire over the heads of their enemies.

10. Pull the trigger. The explosion that follows may leave half your cheek black with soot. And that ringing in your ear may be permanent hearing damage.

11. Quick check—are you dead yet? Nope? Repeat this process.

The Battle of Concord

So much for the Battle of Lexington. Victorious, the British Army presses on to Concord. They arrive and search for the hidden munitions. The rebels recently plowed their fields and buried their ammunition under the furrows of dirt. So the redcoats march right over the ammunition without noticing and proceed

---

* Bayonets are foot-long swords the British attach to the end of their muskets. The British may be charging you with bayonets. If so, you may be dead soon. The Americans do not have bayonets yet. Should have thought of that before you joined the rebels. Next time, genius, bring your iridium blaster.

to search the farmhouses instead. The frustrated redcoats question locals at gunpoint and somehow succeed in burning down the village meeting house. The British toss one hundred barrels of salted food into the town pond, along with 550 pounds of musket balls.[*]

The British divide their troops to cover the bridges entering Concord, because more rebels are pouring in from the countryside. Ninety redcoats guarding the North Bridge are soon outnumbered by four hundred rebel militiamen. The British retreat across the bridge. In their panic, some frightened and exhausted redcoats open fire on the rebels, killing two. (Be careful where you stand during this battle.) The rebels fire back, killing at least two redcoats and wounding eleven. Greatly outnumbered, the British decide it's high time to return to Boston.

More rebels arrive every hour. The rebels soon outnumber the British with one thousand militiamen. They fire on the fleeing British, ambushing and waylaying them at every bridge and bend in the road. The British officers order their soldiers to move faster. Their march breaks into a trot.

As the British cross through the town of Lincoln, the rebel militia swells to two thousand. The British send small attack parties into the surrounding houses and forests. They trap and kill rebels—even rebels who surrender. But the British redcoats have already marched nearly thirty miles since two in the morning and are running out of ammunition.

....

* Don't worry about the polluted pond. After the redcoats leave, the rebels are able to rescue all the musket balls and most of the food, so the British really accomplished precious little in Concord.

Your Odds of Being Hit by a Musket Ball

Both Americans and Brits use the "Brown Bess" musket, which is deadly at fifty yards, but nowhere near as good as a rifle. . . .

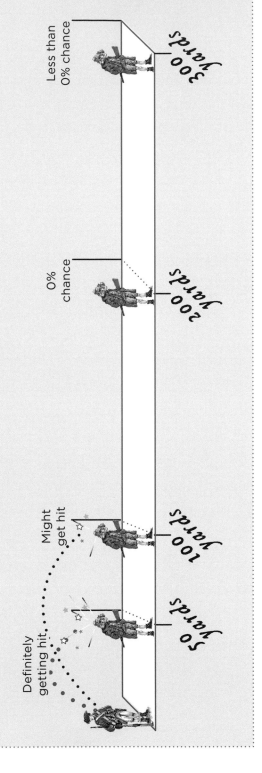

Definitely getting hit

Might get hit

0% chance

Less than 0% chance

50 yards

100 yards

200 yards

300 yards

YOUR ODDS OF BEING HIT BY A RIFLE

Some American rebels use rifles built by German American gunsmiths in Pennsylvania. The inside of a rifle barrel has a spiral groove that spins the bullet as it leaves the gun, increasing range and accuracy.

The British use rifles only for hunting. They don't consider using rifles for warfare, because rifles are complicated to reload, impossible to fit with a bayonet, and a bit pricey. The Americans are the first rifle snipers in the world and will become experts in this deadly art.

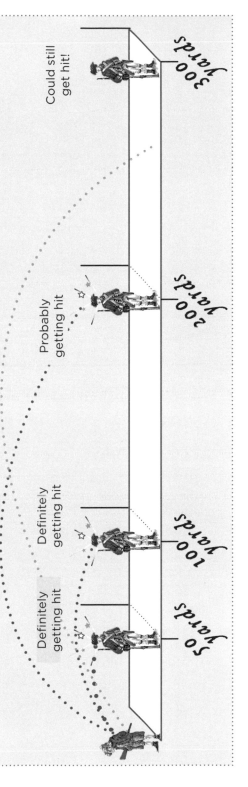

Definitely getting hit

Definitely getting hit

Probably getting hit

Could still get hit!

50 yards

100 yards

200 yards

300 yards

THE BRITISH RETREAT TO BOSTON

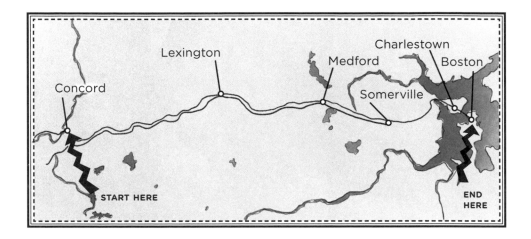

Retreat to Lexington

The British continue to flee. Outside Lexington, the British commander, Lieutenant Colonel Smith, is shot in the thigh. His second in command, Major Pitcairn, is thrown from his bolting horse and injures his arm. The rebel sharpshooters target the British officers. Of all the British officers, only one survives the American assault uninjured. Terrified, the redcoats break ranks and run for Lexington. Under heavy fire, the British officers turn their bayonets on their own men to stop the panicked flight and return order to the troops. The redcoats run out of ammunition.

At 2:30 p.m. the redcoats spot Earl Percy, a British general, arriving with one thousand fresh reinforcements from Boston. Chased by the rebel militia, the British troops run to the safety of Percy's line and collapse with exhaustion. Percy's soldiers march to the tune of "Yankee Doodle" to taunt the rebel Yankees.[*] The redcoats continue their retreat to Boston.

....

[*] Yankee is a word the British use to make fun of the Americans. The song "Yankee Doodle" makes fun of Americans for being foolish, simplistic, and, worst of all, having poor fashion sense.

A company of American senior-citizen militia—veterans over sixty who are too old to serve in the regular militia—ambush a British convoy of supply wagons. They kill several British soldiers, take prisoners, and seize two wagons loaded with ammunition. The American rebels may end the day with more bullets than when they started.

Joseph Warren leads attacks against the retreating British. The redcoats, fearing American snipers, begin clearing every house they encounter on the road—killing civilians, stealing alcohol, and even looting the communion silver from a town church.

By the time the British reach Somerville, the American militia numbers 3,960. The British use their cannon to devastating effect, preventing the rebels from defeating the redcoats. When the exhausted British finally straggle back into Boston, they've marched forty miles and suffered massive losses. Meanwhile, more rebels continue arriving from across the entire colony of Massachusetts. By the following morning, the American rebel army numbers *fifteen thousand* and surrounds the entire city of Boston.* The British Army is trapped. They cannot escape. Their city is under siege by the Americans.

---

* Remember, the entire population of Boston is about fifteen thousand. So it's as if an entire second city of Boston has sprung up overnight.

BATTLES OF LEXINGTON AND ★ CONCORD SCOREBOARD

	British	Americans
Killed:	73	49
Wounded:	174	39
Lost or Deserted:	53	0
Total Losses:	300	88

★ **Winner:** AMERICA

3

THE BATTLE OF BUNKER HILL

You are now going to fight in one of the most terrifying battles of the war. Limber up and maybe take a few multivitamins. Are your affairs in order? Have you written a will? Don't go buying any green bananas—you may not survive the next forty-eight hours.

The British are completely embarrassed to be trapped in Boston. After all, they command the most powerful army on the planet. So the redcoats hatch a plan to capture the hills surrounding Boston Harbor. Once they mount cannons on those hills, they'll be able to bomb the Americans, march out of Boston, and smash the rebellion.

Of course, the Sons of Liberty spies quickly uncover the British secret plan. Joseph Warren, the rebel leader, decides to capture the hills first. This will keep the British trapped in Boston.

On June 16, 1775, the American militia embarks on a daring plan to capture Bunker Hill. They sneak out under the cover of darkness and frantically begin building a fort. They're within the

MAP *of* BUNKER HILL

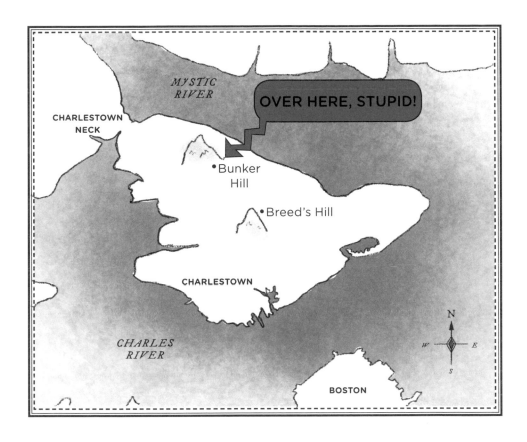

range of British cannons, so they have to work quickly and quietly before they're discovered on the hill. The fort must be complete before sunrise....

The American commanders—lacking knowledge, experience, maps, common sense, and good leadership—somehow build their fort on Breed's Hill by accident. That's right—the Battle of Bunker Hill is actually fought on Breed's Hill.

Get used to these sorts of mistakes—it's going to be a long night. With shovels and picks, you'll help dig a deep fort in the earth, building the dirt up around the edges to make a protective wall . . . on the wrong hill.

At around four in the morning, duck and cover. A British ship spots the American fort and opens fire with cannons. Breed's Hill is a much easier target than Bunker Hill. If you haven't purchased Time Corp life insurance, this may be a good time to consider our affordable rates. The deadly British cannon fire stops the Americans in their tracks.

Luckily, the British leaders are even more incompetent than the Americans in this battle. English admiral Samuel Graves, woken from his sleep by cannon fire that he didn't order, demands that his ships stop firing. This allows the Americans time to complete their fort.

When day breaks, the Americans notice a few problems with their swanky new fort. Namely, it can be attacked from all sides. A few smart commanders assign troops to flank the fort to guard against British attack. The Americans are an amateur militia of shoe cobblers, blacksmiths, farmers, and students. Together, they have about as much military experience as Finn Greenquill's pet jellyfish. If you are into gambling, the smart money is on the British winning this battle. . . .

HELPFUL HINTS:
AFRICAN AMERICANS IN THE REVOLUTIONARY WAR

Three dozen African American soldiers fight in the rebel army at Bunker Hill. Between eight thousand and twelve thousand African Americans eventually join the American side in the Revolution. Many are only allowed to serve in noncombat roles such as builders, wagon drivers, and livestock drovers. But many serve on the front lines and become heroes.

Crispus Attucks, whose father is African and whose mother is Wampanoag American Indian, is the first casualty of the Revolution. He is shot in the Boston Massacre in 1770. Nearly 10 percent of General George Washington's effective fighting force is African American. The First Rhode Island Regiment is 75 percent black. A French officer, observing them on the field, describes the regiment as "the most neatly dressed, the best under arms, and the most precise in its maneuver."

The British have great success recruiting African American slaves into the English ranks by promising them their freedom. This puts pressure on the rebel army to do the same. In these early phases of the war, most of the African Americans fighting for the American rebels are free men. But as the war continues, many slaves will fight for America in exchange for being granted their freedom.

The British Attack

British general Henry Clinton sees the danger in the American advance on Breed's Hill: the rebels will be able to fire cannons directly into Boston. The Americans must be attacked immediately! Clinton realizes the smartest move is to attack the Charlestown Neck, cutting off the Americans and starving them out (see map below). This—it should be noted—is an *excellent* plan.

GENERAL CLINTON'S PLAN

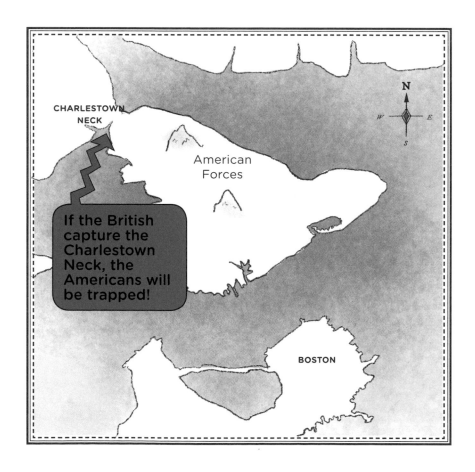

There's just one problem for General Clinton: he is not in charge. A man named General Howe is.* Howe is slow, indecisive, overconfident, and a lousy strategist. It takes him until three in the afternoon to finally launch an attack on the American fort. And his plan is pretty horrendous.

GENERAL HOWE'S NOT-SO-BRILLIANT PLAN:

1. Send British troops up Breed's Hill, directly into American gunfire
2. Get shot at the entire climb
3. ???
4. Victory

Shockingly, General Howe's not-so-brilliant plan does not work. His forces charge uphill, directly into American gunfire. A few minutes later, his forces retreat, some of them full of bullet holes. Meanwhile, British troops—harassed by American sniper fire from the buildings of Charlestown—simply burn down Charlestown. So the Breed's Hill battlefield is now covered in smoke. Since General Howe's attack doesn't work the first time, he gets the idea to try it a second time. Spoiler alert: it still doesn't work.

....
* Howe is pronounced "how," as in, "How did this guy become the commander?"

WORSE COMMANDERS THAN WILLIAM HOWE:

• **Field Marshal Sir Douglas Haig**—British commander who orders 110,000 men to attack impenetrable German trenches during World War I and loses half his men in a single day.

• **The Governor of Lampedusa**—When British Royal Air Force pilot Sidney Cohen runs out of gas and emergency lands on Lampedusa in World War II, he is surprised when all the Italians on the island assume he is attacking and surrender to him.

• **Major G.P.W. Meredith**—The Australian government sends its army to combat an overpopulation of emus in 1932. Emus are flightless birds, and theoretically have no method of escaping the Australian army. Nevertheless, the combined efforts of Major Meredith, the Australian artillery, and ten thousand rounds of machine gun bullets are unable to beat the emus. Meredith withdraws in defeat.

BETTER COMMANDERS THAN WILLIAM HOWE:

- Finn Greenquill's grandmother
- A wet sock
- A bowl of soggy oatmeal
- This book
- A cat stuck in a washing machine

HELPFUL HINTS:
BRITISH BATTLE
"STRATEGY"

If you are fighting on the side of the British, here is a quick explanation of how the British fight battles. Keep in mind, the British Army is the greatest in the world in 1775.

1. Line up in an open field with a close formation that is super easy to shoot at.

2. Wear bright colors such as red to make yourself an easy target.

3. If you are an officer, put on a fancy hat and epaulets and sit on top of a horse. There. You are almost impossible to miss now.

4. March until you are directly in front of the enemy.

5. Fire a weapon that has a high chance of misfiring or missing altogether. Then spend up to thirty seconds attempting to reload it.

6. Repeat step 5 until someone shoots you.

If you're British, the good news is that your enemy is usually as inept as you are. After all, the enemy is fighting with the exact same weapons and tactics. A main reason the British have success in fighting the French and Spanish is that the better-trained British soldiers are faster at reloading their muskets.

The American rebels, observing the fighting style of the American Indians, learn to fire their weapons from behind the cover of trees and stone walls. The British consider these tactics* unfair, though in future wars, they will come to adopt these American methods. Twenty-first-century armies wear camouflage, employ snipers, and never attack in close formations.

* Note: Tactics are not the same thing as Tic Tacs . . . though, when used properly, both are equally sweet.

People to Have Lunch With:
SALEM POOR

Salem Poor is an African American militiaman whose heroism at the Battle of Bunker Hill wins him special recognition by the colony of Massachusetts.

Salem is born into slavery in 1747. He saves his money, and at age twenty-two, buys his freedom for twenty-seven British pounds.*

At age twenty-eight, Salem enlists in the militia. He fights in Captain Benjamin Ames's South Parish Company in the Battle of Bunker Hill. Salem shows exceptional bravery when five soldiers in his regiment are killed next to him and another six are seriously wounded. While other men flee, Salem stays behind to help the wounded. Retreating last, Salem fires the shot that kills British Army lieutenant colonel James

---

* Twenty-seven British pounds is about a year's salary for a workingman in this time period. Or about five years' salary if you're a travel writer for Time Corp.

Abercrombie (the third-ranking British officer on the battlefield).

Fourteen American officers cite Salem for heroism, and petition the General Court of Massachusetts to recognize his valor. Of the thousands of colonists who fight at Bunker Hill, no other soldier is singled out in this manner. Salem goes on to serve throughout the Revolution, surviving Valley Forge and fighting at Saratoga, Monmouth, and the Battle of White Plains. He is discharged on March 20, 1780.

Salem is married four times. In 1771, he marries a half–American Indian servant named Nancy Parker. In 1780, he marries Mary Twing, a free African American. In 1787, he marries a white woman named Sarah Stevens. And in 1799, he marries a final time, though nothing is known of this last wife.[*]

Americans Fight to the Death

Joseph Warren, though a Major General of the American rebels, chooses to serve on the front lines of Breed's Hill. The Americans are nearly out of ammunition, so every bullet must count. The order is given: "Don't fire until you see the whites of their eyes!"

---

[*] Not much is known about what happened to all of Salem Poor's wives. But if you meet Salem Poor's divorce attorney, Finn Greenquill wants to hire him.

The Americans, baking in their fort in the scorching summer sun, have no food or water. They are filthy from a night of digging in the dirt and being pounded by British cannons. But they do not cut and run. They hold their line and keep fighting. Peter Salem, an African American minuteman*, mortally wounds British marine major Pitcairn with his final bullet.

HELPFUL HINTS:
WHAT TO DO IF YOU ARE SHOT BY A MUSKET

1. Don't panic.

2. Okay, maybe panic.

3. Scream for the nearest field medic. Joseph Warren, for instance, is a doctor.

4. Okay, there's good news and bad news. Okay, actually it's all bad news. It's 1775. Surgery is very primitive. The doctor will probably amputate a leg or an arm, and you'll feel all of it. Anesthetic is not invented yet. All the doctor can do for the pain is tell you to bite down on a musket ball or a leather strap. Occasionally, doctors will distract patients from the pain by having the army's drummer play loudly in their ears.[†]

* Historians believe Peter Salem may have been one of several Muslims fighting in the American Revolution. They aren't sure; if you see him, you'll have to ask him. Salem goes on to serve in the Continental Army for five years, so you'll have a chance to run into him.

[†] This is actually true.

5. How are you enjoying your Time Corp vacation so far?

6. So you've survived your field amputation. You'll probably get an infection and die because washing your hands before surgery is not discovered until 1847.

7. We hope you have enjoyed your vacation with Time Corp. Remember, no refunds—all vacation sales are final!

The Final Assault

General Howe attacks for the third and final time. He uses the exact same tactics that failed the first two times. Only now the Americans are out of ammunition and must fight with their bare hands. The British have bayonets—a huge advantage. A puncture wound from a bayonet is often far worse than a musket ball (so, if you get shot, just be glad you're not being bayoneted). Outnumbered and out of bullets, the Americans are slaughtered. Joseph Warren, the rebel leader and president of the Massachusetts Congress, is killed on the front lines.[*]

---

[*] On March 21, 1776, Dr. Warren's friends search the battlefield and find his body in a hastily dug grave. The decomposed body is unrecognizable, but Paul Revere—as a silversmith—is able to identify Warren from a silver false tooth Revere made for him. So, in the end, Revere and his friends are able to give Joseph Warren a proper funeral in a marked grave.

	British	Americans
Killed:	226	115
Wounded:	828	305
Total Losses:	1054	420

★ **Winner:** BRITAIN

All told, the British lose nearly a hundred commanding officers to injuries or death. And the British suffer more than twice as many casualties as the Americans. Technically, the British win the battle. But as General Clinton later writes in his diary, "A few more such victories would have shortly put an end to British dominion in America."

4

THE SIEGE OF BOSTON

If you're still alive, you're probably wishing you purchased one of Time Corp's safer vacation packages. Perhaps our tropical dinosaur-hunting safari in the Jurassic period, or else our relaxing beach getaway to the pirate-infested waters of the seventeenth-century Caribbean. Either way, Time Corp vacations are nonrefundable. So you'd better reload your musket and look sharp. You're about to meet General George Washington, help form the first American army, and attack the British in Boston.

The hastily formed Continental Congress names forty-three-year-old George Washington the commander in chief of the newly formed Continental Army. He arrives in Boston in July 1775 to take command of the siege. He's six foot two and strikingly handsome, with reddish hair and piercing blue eyes. The soft-spoken Virginian has star power. (Time Corp tried to sign him to an endorsement deal but couldn't meet his quote.)

George Washington has battle experience from the French and Indian War. The French and Indian War is pretty much what

it sounds like: the French teamed up with the American Indians to go to war against the British colonies. Here's the thing—and this is a bit awkward—George Washington pretty much single-handedly caused the French and Indian War.

Yes, it was a young Lieutenant Colonel George Washington who ambushed and butchered a group of French Canadians in Pennsylvania back in 1754. This little misunderstanding came to be known as the Battle of Jumonville Glen. It enraged the French, plunged America into the French and Indian War, and led France and Britain into the Seven Years' War.[*] Oops.

What's even more awkward for George Washington is that the French and Indian War kinda caused the American Revolu-

....

* The Seven Years' War is, amazingly, a war that lasts roughly seven years. It starts with France and England fighting over territory in America. But eventually the war sucks in nearly every country in Europe and is fought on battlefields across five continents. Thanks, George Washington!

tion. The British kinda raised taxes on the Americans to pay for the expensive French and Indian War. So the French and Indian War, the Seven Years' War, and the entire Revolutionary War are all kinda George Washington's fault.

Nevertheless, Washington's four years of military experience give him more military experience than virtually any other soldier in the rebel army. The only real problem is Washington doesn't want the job. He's one of the richest men in the thirteen colonies. He doesn't think the Americans can win, and he prefers to stay on his massive Virginia farm, counting his money.

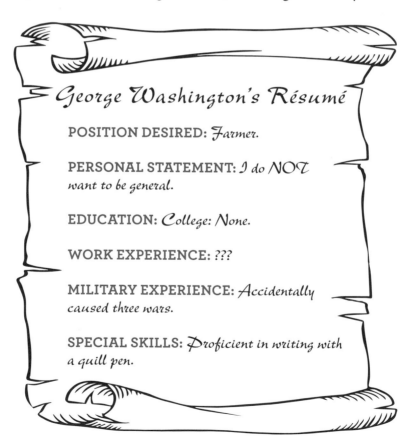

George Washington's Résumé

POSITION DESIRED: Farmer.

PERSONAL STATEMENT: I do NOT want to be general.

EDUCATION: College: None.

WORK EXPERIENCE: ???

MILITARY EXPERIENCE: Accidentally caused three wars.

SPECIAL SKILLS: Proficient in writing with a quill pen.

Washington is not very qualified. But he does have one point in his favor: all the other candidates for the job are *even less* qualified. When future president John Adams nominates Washington to command the Continental Army, Washington feels it's his duty to accept. This is not an easy decision. The British make it clear that all rebel leaders will be hung from a scaffold as traitors to the British Crown.[*]

When George Washington arrives in Boston, he is so depressed at the shabby state of the Continental Army that he considers quitting before he even starts. The army has no discipline. Soldiers drink and fight. Sickness ravages the camp because the untrained soldiers don't know to dig latrines.[†] There is almost no gunpowder whatsoever. Two thousand American soldiers do not even have muskets. Troops desert every day as they go hungry or simply decide to walk home to tend their farms.

Meanwhile, the siege on Boston is a stalemate. The poorly trained rebels aren't strong enough to push the British Army out of Boston. All they can do is keep the British surrounded. If George Washington wants to free the people of Boston from the redcoats, he's going to need a miracle. . . .

....

[*] Finn Greenquill has forced us to step in here and make it clear that the British aren't all bad. Just because they're all-powerful overlords doesn't make them evil. Fully one-third of the British government votes against going to war with America. Edmund Burke, a possible time traveler, is a member of the British government who correctly predicts the entire outcome of the war. Burke sees a future in which America becomes a wealthy and powerful country, and he thinks it's wiser for England to keep on good terms with America.

[†] Latrines are toilet pits, dug in the ground. The reason they are important is if several thousand men go to the bathroom in your army camp without first digging a pit, you're going to have a bad time. Suffice it to say, if you join Washington's army, bring a clothespin for your nose, a positive mental attitude, and a lot of toilet paper.

PRANKING THE PAST

If you want to really cheer up George Washington, transport some elite Navy SEALs to 1775. A few machine guns and rocket launchers might help even the score against the British.

If that doesn't work, you can always transport a rampaging horde of Mongol horse archers into downtown Boston. That ought to keep the British on their toes.

People to Have Lunch With:
JOHN GREENWOOD

John Greenwood is a sixteen-year-old soldier in Washington's newly formed Continental Army. He was friends with Samuel Maverick, a seventeen-year-old shot by the British at the Boston Massacre. When John hears the news of the Battles of Lexington and Concord, he walks alone, 150 miles, from Maine to Boston to join the rebel army.

John stops in taverns along the way and plays his fife. When people ask him where he is going, he tells them he is going to fight for his country. He is not the only boy to enlist. For instance, in northern New Jersey, nearly 75 percent of boys aged fifteen and sixteen join the Continental Army. One continental soldier,

Israel Trask, is only ten years old, and serves as a messenger. Artilleryman Jeremiah Levering enters the service at age twelve. Thousands of Continental soldiers are under age twenty.

When the Americans lose the Battle of Bunker Hill, John Greenwood sees the bleeding patriots limping back to Cambridge. Discouraged, he considers leaving the service. But he happens to meet an injured African American who plans to return to battle after healing from his wounds. The man's courage inspires Greenwood to continue in the army.

Greenwood will eventually become George Washington's dentist and fit the leader with his famous dentures. Despite popular belief, Washington's dentures—as it happens—are not made of wood. They are carved from hippopotamus tusk.

Robbing Fort Ticonderoga

It's time for you to participate in a heist.

First, set your Time Corp Time Machine Colonial™ for May 10, 1775, and march with Benedict Arnold and Ethan Allen as their eighty-three troops, known as the Green Mountain Boys, launch a surprise attack on the British at Fort Ticonderoga in northern New York. The Green Mountain Boys catch the British while they are still sleeping, and capture the fort without a fight.

Now, General Washington needs cannons if he's going to

chase the British Army out of Boston and free the city. This leads a young Boston bookseller named Henry Knox to land on a crazy idea. Why not haul all the captured cannons from Fort Ticonderoga three hundred miles down to Boston? How hard could it possibly be? George Washington, willing to try anything at this point, gives Knox the thumbs-up.

The Trail of Henry Knox

Henry Knox is a big, round, cheerful man with a sense of humor. And a good thing too—he's had a rough couple of years. When he was twenty-two, he accidentally blew two fingers off his left hand with a shotgun. Then he was forced to flee Boston when the British took over. The British destroyed his bookstore and all of his books. Now twenty-four, Henry's life will not get easier any-time soon. . . .

In November, Henry loots Fort Ticonderoga, taking cannons, mortars, and howitzers. Altogether, the cannons weigh 119,000 pounds. These include the "Big Berthas," five-thousand-pound cannons that are eleven feet long and fire a twenty-four-pound cannonball. You can join Henry on this raid, but you may want to skip the next couple of months of his journey—it ain't pretty.

Henry's first day of moving the cannons goes pretty well, but on his second day, one of his cannon boats sinks in Lake George. Through a heroic effort, Henry is able to bail out the ship and rescue the cannons. We should mention he's doing most of this in December, in the dead of winter. By December 17, there is enough snow for Henry's men to build forty-two sleds, dragging the cannons with eighty yoke of oxen.

KNOX'S TRIP *of* HARD KNOCKS

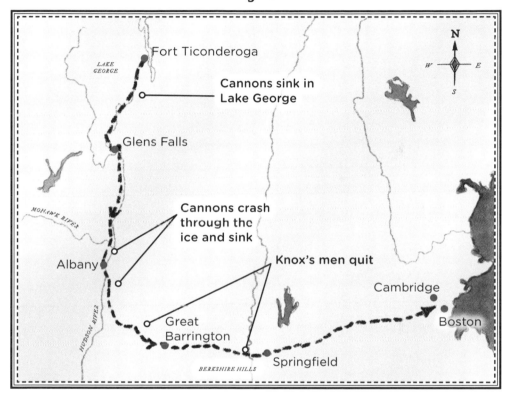

When Henry reaches the Hudson River, the ice is not yet thick enough to cross. He and his men pour water over the ice to thicken it. Twice, the cannons crash through the ice and fall in the freezing river. Henry Knox fishes them out every time. If you are serving on his crew, you have our sympathies. Also, happy holidays!

Henry schleps the cannons through the Berkshire Hills. On

January 9, his crew refuses to keep going. They quit and go home to New York. Henry has to hire new men and fresh oxen. It is on January 27, 1776, that Henry Knox finally delivers the cannons to General Washington in Cambridge. The total job took ten weeks and cost 521 pounds.* But Henry does not lose a single cannon on the three-hundred-mile journey.

PRANKING THE PAST

Just when Henry Knox rolls his last cannon into Cambridge . . . transport them all back to Fort Ticonderoga.

HELPFUL HINTS:

WHAT TO EXPECT WHEN YOU'RE EXPECTING . . . TO BE SHOT BY A CANNON

1. If you're on a battlefield and you hear a deafening boom, you may be being shot at by a cannon.

2. If you hear a loud whistling sound, that is the cannonball flying straight toward you.

---

* This is actually an amazing bargain, considering how much it costs to manufacture British cannons.

3. Do not try to outrun the cannonball; it travels eight hundred feet per second, and you don't.

4. Remain calm. There is nothing to be afraid of, aside from death.

5. Shout and wave your arms to make yourself appear larger, to intimidate the cannonball. Oh wait, no. That's if you're attacked by a mountain lion.

6. Quietly back away slowly. Oh wait, sorry. That's if you're charged by a bear.

7. Okay, hang on. Let us think for a second.

8. All right, there's really nothing you can do. Maybe start to panic.

9. Do you have an iridium blaster? Well, that won't help. No one can hit a target moving at eight hundred feet per second.

10. Is this a good time to remind you to purchase Time Corp's very affordable life insurance package for only $999,999,999*?

11. If you feel a slight twinge in your side, like your body is being torn in half, you may be being hit by a cannonball.

12. You probably should have chosen a different vacation package. Thank you for time traveling with Time Corp, where every good decision is made in hindsight.

---

* With mail-in rebate.

Cannons Are Awesome

A large cannon will fire a cannonball nearly a mile. If the cannonball doesn't kill you on impact, it can kill you on the bounce. A cannonball bouncing through ranks of soldiers in an infantry square can kill dozens. If a cannonball is fired directly into a column of advancing soldiers, it can pass straight through up to forty men. Washington finally has the cannons he needs. This is huge. It's time to put them to work against the British.

Sneaking the Cannons into Position

Set your Time Corp Time Machine Colonial™ for March 4, 1776. Under the cloak of night, you can help General Washington's Continental Army sneak Henry Knox's cannons onto Dorchester Heights. Two thousand patriot workers and 360 oxcarts lug equipment up the hill. Hay bales are placed between the troops

HENRY KNOX'S CANNONS
FIND A NEW HOME

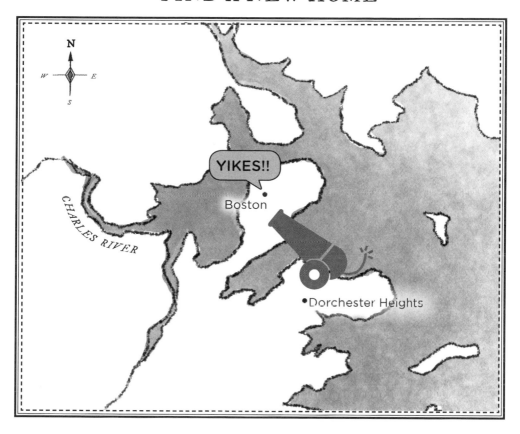

and the harbor in order to stifle the sounds of the moving cannons. Wagon wheels are muffled with straw. General Washington gallops up and down the lines, whispering encouragement to the soldiers. Miraculously, by four in the morning, all the cannon batteries are complete. The Americans can now rain leaden terror down into Boston.

People to Have Lunch With:
PHILLIS WHEATLEY

While you are in Boston in March 1776, be sure to drop in when General George Washington invites Phillis Wheatley to lunch. Phillis Wheatley is only twenty-three and already the most famous poet in Boston. She is also the first published African American woman poet.

Phillis is born in West Africa. At age seven she is captured, sold into slavery, and shipped to America. A wealthy Boston merchant named John Wheatley buys her as a servant for his wife, Susanna. They name her Phillis after the slave ship that carried her over from Africa. The Wheatley family recognizes Phillis's brilliance and gives her an education that's unusual for women of that time. By age twelve, Phillis is fluent in Greek and Latin. By age fourteen, she's composing her own poetry. By age twenty, she is touring London and meeting with lords and countesses who are fans of her work.

In 1778, when John Wheatley dies, Phillis will be freed from slavery. In this time period, it is nearly impossible to make a living as a poet. In fact, it's nearly impossible in any time period. Phillis will become a scullery maid. She falls into poverty and dies in 1784 at the age of thirty-one.

Winning the Siege

The British wake up on the morning of March 5 to discover Knox's guns staring down at them from Dorchester Heights. It's like the overnight trick the Americans pulled at Breed's Hill, except this time, it totally, totally works. All of Boston is now threatened by American guns. The astonished British general William Howe is heard saying, "The rebels have done more in one night than my whole army could do in months."

The British know they must flee. They offer Washington a deal: they won't spitefully burn Boston to the ground as long as they're allowed to retreat without being attacked by American cannons. Washington agrees. Eleven thousand British soldiers and sailors abandon Boston and set sail for Nova Scotia to regroup their army and plot their next assault on the American rebels.

When Washington's army marches into Boston after the nine-month siege, many Bostonians are finally able to return to their homes. They find their city torn apart and vandalized. The British have used the Old South Meeting House, where the Boston Tea Party began, as a place to race horses. The rebels will be left with a huge cleaning bill. But they also discover blankets, medical supplies, and sixty-nine much-needed cannons. The Continental Army is growing. . . .

5
THE DECLARATION OF INDEPENDENCE

Thomas Jefferson

You've worked pretty hard and probably need a break from all the constant battles. Why not powder your wig and head over to Philadelphia to watch the signing of the Declaration of Independence on July 4, 1776?

A congress of representatives from the thirteen colonies meets in Philadelphia and decides it's high time to formally declare separation from Britain. The declaration is drafted by a thirty-three-year-old Virginian landowner named Thomas Jefferson.

Like Washington, Jefferson is handsome, six foot two, and won't sign any endorsement deals with Time Corp.

It is Jefferson who hammers out the immortal words of the declaration (with a few copy edits by Benjamin Franklin):

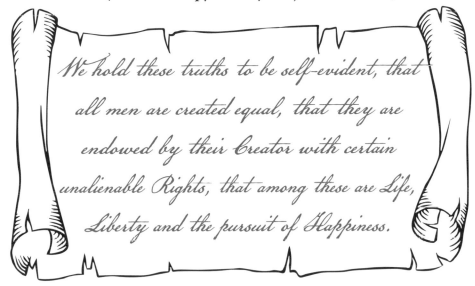

We hold these truths to be self-evident, that all men are created equal, that they are endowed by their Creator with certain unalienable Rights, that among these are Life, Liberty and the pursuit of Happiness.

The idea that all men are equal and have a right to freedom is pretty nifty. In fact, it's one of the first times in human history that anyone thinks to start a government founded on freedom and equality. The Americans don't want to be ruled by kings, but by ideas.

Still, there are a few small caveats. Notice that Jefferson only says that all *men* are created equal. In 1776, women have the right to do the cooking and the laundry, and that's about it. American women won't get the right to vote until 1920.

As far as liberty, African Americans don't win that right until 1865. While there are free African Americans in 1776, the majority are still slaves. Jefferson himself owns more than six hundred slaves over the course of his life. Many of the Founding Fathers despise slavery. John Adams is furious that the declaration claims all men are created equal while not granting freedom to the slaves. He believes that history will never forgive the Founding Fathers for this hypocrisy. Still, while the declaration may not be perfect, it is a step in the right direction, paving the way toward a nation that will be based on freedom and equality.

Set foot in the Pennsylvania State House on 520 Chestnut Street in downtown Philadelphia on July 4, 1776, and you will witness one of the most important moments in American history. The Continental Congress votes on and passes the declaration—announcing to the world that America is now independent from Britain. This is the first moment America calls itself a free country.

Looking around the room, you may notice how young the Founding Fathers are. The average age of the signers is forty-four, with a dozen men under thirty-five.[*]

After the president of the Congress, John Hancock, smacks his unusually large signature on the declaration, you may hear him tell the group, "We must now all hang together." Benjamin Franklin quickly replies, "Yes, we must indeed all hang together, or most assuredly we shall all hang separately."

....

[*] Compare this with the year 2016, when the average age of US senators is sixty-three and the youngest senator is forty. Or compare this with the year 2164, when the average US senator is 153 and the youngest senator is a robot.

People to Have Lunch With:
BENJAMIN FRANKLIN

Benjamin Franklin is one of the most interesting people in history. His ideas are so ahead of his time, Franklin is almost definitely a time traveler.* He serves as the US ambassador to France and is also America's most famous scientist and writer in the 1700s.

Franklin is born on January 17, 1706, the fifteenth out of a whopping seventeen children. At age ten, he is forced to leave school and go to work. Rising from a childhood of poverty and physical abuse, by age forty Franklin has taught himself French and Italian and become one of the wealthiest men in Pennsylvania. He retires from his printing business young so he can devote all his time to scientific discovery. Many of his

---

* If you do manage to score a lunch date with Franklin, note that he is a vegetarian.

inventions (listed below) change the lives of people in the 1700s.

When Benjamin Franklin dies on April 17, 1790, at the age of eighty-four, twenty thousand people attend the funeral. As further proof that he's a time traveler, Franklin will create bank accounts in Boston and Philadelphia that are sealed for centuries. Two hundred years after his death, the $8,800 he invested in each savings account grows to $6.5 million. Part of this giant sum of money is given to local students for scholarships.

A full biography of Benjamin Franklin would fill several books, and unfortunately, Finn Greenquill doesn't pay us by the word. So here is a brief list of just a few of . . .

BENJAMIN FRANKLIN'S INVENTIONS, DISCOVERIES, AND ACCOMPLISHMENTS

- Bifocals
- The Franklin stove (which heats a house better than a fireplace)
- The rocking chair
- The electrical battery
- The flexible catheter (used for surgery)
- The lightning rod
- A musical instrument called a glass armonica (both Mozart and Beethoven compose music for this instrument)

- The pro and con list
- Starts the first American lending library
- Starts the first American fire department
- Proves that lightning is electricity
- Discovers and names electrical concepts such as "conductor," "current," and "capacitor"
- Discovers the Atlantic Gulf Stream, saving time on ocean voyages
- Starts the University of Pennsylvania
- Serves as a congressman, the postmaster general, and ambassador to France

What have YOU done lately?

HELPFUL HINTS:
AMERICAN INDIANS IN THE AMERICAN REVOLUTION

If you read the fine print on the Declaration of Independence, you may notice Jefferson refers to "the merciless Indian Savages, whose known rule of warfare, is an undistinguished destruction of all ages, sexes and conditions." Again, you may scratch your chin wondering how Jefferson could write that "all men are created equal" while also referring to "merciless Indian Savages."

The American Indians have fought with white settlers for a hundred years. This is why Jefferson isn't a fan. The problem is, the British and American settlers keep taking American Indian land, while the American Indians keep wanting to stay alive. All this means that when the American Revolution breaks out, the American Indians don't know which side to fight on.

In western Massachusetts, Stockbridge Indians volunteer as militiamen, join the Continental Army at the siege of Boston, and serve alongside George Washington in New York and New Jersey. Meanwhile, Cherokee warriors, angry about losing their land, help the British by attacking the colonies in the south (and are defeated in Virginia, Georgia, and the Carolinas).

The Revolution divides the Iroquois tribes into a civil war. Some Iroquois, like the Mohawks, stay loyal to the British, while other Iroquois tribes, like the Oneidas, side with the Americans. The Iroquois end up fighting each other at the Battle of Oriskany in 1777.

Ohio Indians pledge a peace treaty with the Americans, which American soldiers break by murdering two of their leaders: Cornstalk of the Shawnees and White Eyes of the Delawares. Because of this, the Ohio Indians switch sides to the British and go on to fight the Americans for a dozen years after the end of the Revolutionary War.

Ultimately, Britain will give all the American Indian land to the United States in a peace treaty. So whether

American Indians support the British or the Americans doesn't really matter; they will lose pretty much all their land anyway. Several time travelers have tried to warn the American Indians of this, but unfortunately, we are not allowed to change the course of history. All we can do is try to be better people in the future.

Riots in New York

The Declaration of Independence is copied and spread throughout the thirteen colonies. When it reaches New York City on July 9, 1776, it causes a riot. George Washington marches his troops to the city green to hear the declaration read. The enthusiastic crowd, whipped into a frenzy of patriotic fervor, tears down a nearby statue of King George III. They cut off the statue's head and mount it on a spike in front of the local tavern. The rest of the statue is melted down and molded into more than forty-two thousand musket balls, to be put to use against the British.

A few of the 1776 copies of the Declaration of Independence still exist. One will be found by a Philadelphia man in 1989, who discovers it hidden in the back of a picture frame he picks up at a flea market for four dollars. It's in perfect condition and sells at auction for $8.1 million in 2000. If you find any other copies of the Declaration of Independence, please notify Finn Greenquill—he'll give you a good price.

TIME CORP!™ SERVING YESTERDAY, FOR A BETTER TOMORROW, TODAY.™

A MESSAGE FROM THE GOOD PEOPLE AT THE TIME PATROL

Time Patrol Officer Ned McGillicutty here! His Eminence, Mr. Greenquill, demanded I write something. That's fine, it's not as if I have seven thousand years' worth of cleanup work to do, thanks to you loudmouthed, troublemaking time travelers.

When you go camping, did you ever hear the phrase "leave no trace"? Apparently not, because all you time travelers want to do is create gigantic messes to history's timeline. Just last week, a group of you teleported a two-hundred-ton blue whale into the Latona Fountain at Versailles, right in the middle of the French Revolution. Who had to clean that up? Ned McGillicutty, that's who.

Then a bunch of you had a sleepover in Catherine the Great's Pavlovsk Palace and completely trashed the place. Nearly a hundred rooms, and all covered in Silly String. Well, you are not getting your security deposit back, I can tell you that much!

And I hate to say it, but I am sick to death of everyone taking potshots at Joseph Stalin. Look, nobody loves a murderous dictator, but we're not allowed to change the past, all right? Every time you fire a sniper round at Stalin, guess who has to leap in and take the bullet? You guessed it: Ned McGillicutty. Even with a bulletproof vest on, you know how it feels to take a bullet for Stalin? Pretty lousy.

So think about this the next time you mess around in history. Oh, and Mr. Greenquill says I should thank you for traveling with Time Corp, and funding his giant diamond collection.

Ned

Ned McGillicutty
Time Patrol Agent

6

THE BATTLE OF BROOKLYN

Make sure your boots are buckled tightly, because you're about to spend the next few days on the run. The British Army is coming, and this time they're not messing around. The Brits need to destroy the American resistance and stamp out this rebellion once and for all.

With Boston freed, General Washington moves his rebel army to defend New York City—the largest and most important city on the coast. Starting in April 1776, his army spends months building forts and defenses.

Finally, in August, the British Royal Navy sails down from Canada and attacks New York with the largest water-to-land assault of the eighteenth century. Four hundred navy ships, including seventy-three warships, sail into New York's harbor. No one in America has ever seen such an enormous fleet. Each warship is a floating fortress, bristling with dozens of cannons and hundreds of marines. One astonished American soldier, Daniel McCurtin, wakes one morning to see so many British ship masts filling the harbor, he says the bay resembles "a wood of pine trees. . . . I thought all London was afloat."

The British Army musters thirty-two thousand soldiers, including eight thousand Hessian mercenaries. The Hessians are highly skilled German soldiers who work for British coin.* General William Howe commands the British Army, and his big brother, Admiral Richard Howe, commands the navy.[†]

Before you attempt to defend New York from the British, Time Corp's legal department wants to make sure you fully understand the risks. In 1776, the British military is the best in history—better than Caesar's Roman army that conquered Western Europe, better than Genghis Khan's horde that conquered Asia.

Britain has the most powerful navy in the world. Period. In 1773, after England vastly expands its territory in the Seven Years' War, it is said that the sun never sets on the British Empire.

New York is not the healthiest place for you to be right now. George Washington orders the city evacuated. Eighty percent of the citizens flee to the countryside. The New York City population plummets from twenty-five thousand to five thousand people. The only good news is, once the cannonballs start flying, you can get a hotel room really cheap.

....

* Finn Greenquill hires Hessian soldiers to hunt down anyone who owes outstanding bills to Time Corp. He highly recommends hiring Hessian mercenaries. They are terrifying fighters and well worth the price. Have you ever heard of the Headless Horseman from "The Legend of Sleepy Hollow"? According to the story, the Headless Horseman is a Hessian mercenary.

† Admiral Howe is a member of the British government. It should be noted that he voted against the Intolerable Acts. So while he's a great naval commander, he's not necessarily a bad guy.

PRANKING THE PAST

TEN BEST WAYS TO SAVE
NEW YORK FROM THE ROYAL NAVY

10. If the Royal Navy stops for directions, send them to New Jersey.

9. Replace all their gunpowder with sneezing powder. Replace their cannonballs with beach balls.

8. Transport the Royal Navy to the Sahara. If that doesn't work, transport the Sahara to the Royal Navy.

7. Two words: Chuck Norris.

6. Give the entire Royal Navy smart phones. They'll become so distracted, they'll forget all about attacking New York.

5. Transport their uniforms to a different century. Replace them with cheerleader outfits.

4. Say hello to my iridium blaster.

3. Send the Royal Navy a yoga instructor. Teach them mindfulness.

2. Play electronic dance music until they throw themselves overboard.

1. Four hundred Royal Navy ships . . . meet four hundred and one velociraptors.

BEST ARMIES IN THE WORLD, 1776[*]

1. Great Britain	11. Sweden
2. Spain	12. Algeria
3. France	13. Japan
4. Portugal	14. Italian States
5. China	15. Ethiopia
6. Russia	16. Afghanistan
7. Holy Roman Empire	. . .
8. Ottoman Empire	89. Tahiti
9. Netherlands	90. Fiji
10. Persia	91. America

The British Attack Brooklyn

On August 22, General Howe lands fifteen thousand British troops on Long Island. He soon adds five thousand Hessian mercenaries. They march toward Brooklyn, killing cattle and burning every farmhouse in their path. General Washington attempts to defend Brooklyn. But the British outnumber him more than two to one. Washington is outflanked, outmaneuvered, and outgunned.

Hessian mercenaries smash the American line like a tidal wave, skewering patriots with their bayonets. The desperate

....

[*] Note: These rankings are based on empire size, military size, military victories, technology, and Finn Greenquill's personal opinions.

Americans—still with no bayonets—swing their muskets and rifles like clubs, fighting for their lives in hand-to-hand combat. Many Americans who throw down their weapons in surrender are bayoneted by the German mercenaries anyway. One thousand Americans are captured and packed aboard prison ships.

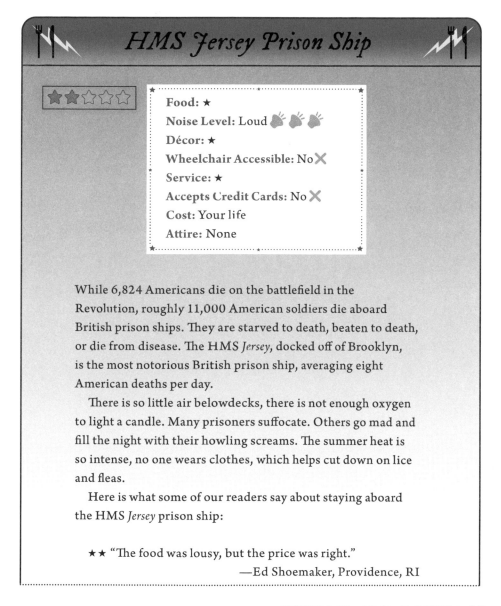

HMS Jersey Prison Ship

★★☆☆☆

Food: ★
Noise Level: Loud 👏 👏 👏
Décor: ★
Wheelchair Accessible: No ✗
Service: ★
Accepts Credit Cards: No ✗
Cost: Your life
Attire: None

While 6,824 Americans die on the battlefield in the Revolution, roughly 11,000 American soldiers die aboard British prison ships. They are starved to death, beaten to death, or die from disease. The HMS *Jersey*, docked off of Brooklyn, is the most notorious British prison ship, averaging eight American deaths per day.

There is so little air belowdecks, there is not enough oxygen to light a candle. Many prisoners suffocate. Others go mad and fill the night with their howling screams. The summer heat is so intense, no one wears clothes, which helps cut down on lice and fleas.

Here is what some of our readers say about staying aboard the HMS *Jersey* prison ship:

★★ "The food was lousy, but the price was right."
—Ed Shoemaker, Providence, RI

Brooklyn Heights

Admiral Howe's personal secretary, Ambrose Serle, is unimpressed with the amateur American troops. He describes Washington's Continental Army as "old men of sixty, boys of fourteen, and blacks of all ages and ragged for the most part." The Americans are beaten all the way across Brooklyn until they are cornered at Brooklyn Heights. There is only one thing that can save the Americans now: the incompetence of British general Howe. Howe decides to call off the attack, surround the Americans, and attempt to starve them out.

General Washington realizes his feeble army is not yet a match for the British. The Americans have no choice but to escape across the East River into Manhattan. There's just one problem: the East River is patrolled by the British Royal Navy—the most deadly navy in the world.

At 9:00 p.m., Washington orders every boat he can muster to begin ferrying his soldiers across the East River under the cover of darkness. Wagon wheels are muffled, and soldiers

BATTLE OF BROOKLYN

are forbidden to speak. Soldiers of the Pennsylvania regiment tend hundreds of campfires to convince the British that the Continental Army is still on the Brooklyn Heights.*

When the sun rises the next day, you may notice that not all of Washington's troops made it safely across in time. A miracle saves the remaining American soldiers: a thick fog rolls in and blankets the East River. The last soldiers are able to flee in boats

---

* It's sort of amazing how many times the British fall for this trick throughout the Revolutionary War. The Americans will successfully pull this exact same stunt again the night before the Battle of Princeton in January 1777.

across the river after sunrise without the British noticing. General Washington is the last man to step into the last boat. Washington's army of nine thousand soldiers safely escapes to Manhattan.

The British Attack Manhattan

General Howe once again ignores brilliant advice from poor General Clinton. Clinton, who strategized the successful British attack in Brooklyn, suggests the British sail up to the Bronx and land there, trapping the Americans on the island of Manhattan. Howe rejects this good advice and dillydallies until September 15, 1776, before landing directly on Manhattan at Kip's Bay.

Hold on to your hat. At 11:00 a.m., five British warships pound the Continental Army's defenses into smithereens. Forts and walls that took the rebels months to build are destroyed in a matter of minutes. Eighty guns fire at the rebels for one hour, burying the Americans under sand and rubble. British transport ships appear out of the smoke, and land nine thousand troops on the shore of Manhattan. The rebel soldiers panic and run.

George Washington gallops his horse among his fleeing men, cursing their cowardice. He cocks his pistol and draws his sword, screaming at his rebel militia to stay and fight. He smacks panicked soldiers with his riding crop. When all of his soldiers scamper away in retreat, Washington throws his hat to the ground and shouts, "Are these the men with which I am to defend America?"

The Hessians attack, shooting and bayoneting American

MAP *of* MANHATTAN

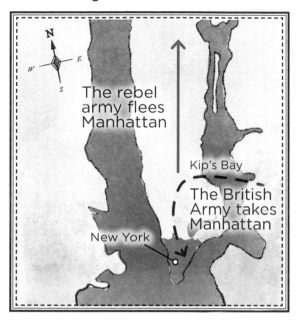

The rebel army flees Manhattan

Kip's Bay

The British Army takes Manhattan

New York

troops trying to surrender. One Hessian cuts off an American soldier's head and mounts it on a pole. The Americans are routed, running for their lives across Manhattan. Unless you have an iridium blaster, you'd better run, too.

General Howe takes control of New York City, raising the British flag in the town commons where the Declaration of Independence was read just a few months ago. Howe now performs his signature move: he stops. He orders a halt to the invasion while he waits for additional troops to arrive. This surprisingly poor choice allows General Washington time to marshal his men in Harlem Heights at the top of Manhattan.

There Washington's troops are able to cross the East River and escape the island of Manhattan. At Throgs Point, twenty-five American riflemen successfully defend a key bridge, preventing four thousand British soldiers from advancing and cutting off the American line of retreat. Howe has the chance to trap the rebel army in Manhattan and win the war, but he blows it. Granted, New York will be held by the British for another seven years. But Washington's army, beaten and bloodied, lives to fight another day.

★ BATTLE OF BROOKLYN SCOREBOARD ★

	British	Americans
Killed:	64	300
Injured:	293	700
Missing or Captured:	31	1,000
Total Losses:	388	2,000

★ **Winner:** BRITAIN

The British vandalize New York City, even burning books. On September 21, one-quarter of New York—five hundred buildings—is burned to the ground in an arsonist's fire.* George Washington asks for spies to volunteer to stay in the occupied city. Only one man volunteers: a twenty-one-year-old Yale graduate named Lieutenant Nathan Hale. But after just ten days of spying, Hale is caught, questioned by General William Howe, and hung. Hale's last words are, "I only regret that I have but one life to lose for my country."

....

* The Great Fire of New York is a tragedy for everyone except Finn Greenquill. After building his first time machine, Finn purchased the future property of Time Corp in 1776 at fire sale prices. No one knows who started the Great Fire of New York, but Finn Greenquill insists it wasn't him.

The British chase Washington's Continental Army across the colonies of New York and New Jersey. They whip the Americans in battle after battle. On November 16, Washington weeps as he watches the British capture Fort Washington (named after him), taking three thousand American prisoners. In despair, more of General Washington's soldiers desert in droves. By December 1776, the Americans have all but lost the war. . . .

NUMBER *of* SOLDIERS *in the* CONTINENTAL ARMY,
December 1775–December 1776

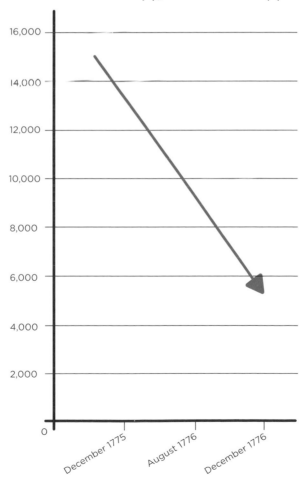

CONFIDENCE *of the* CONTINENTAL ARMY,
December 1775–December 1776

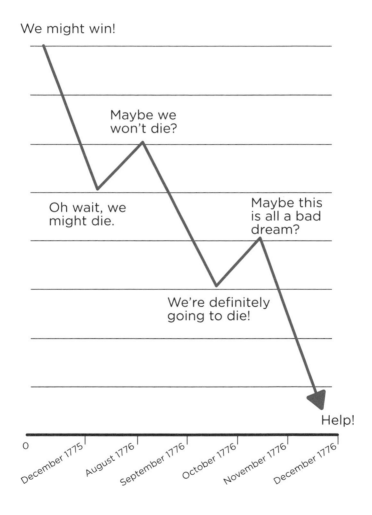

We might win!

Maybe we won't die?

Oh wait, we might die.

Maybe this is all a bad dream?

We're definitely going to die!

Help!

0

December 1775   August 1776   September 1776   October 1776   November 1776   December 1776

7
THE CRISIS

Okay, we're not going to sugarcoat it: things are looking really bad for the Americans. Washington's soldiers are starving and shoeless. You can tell where the Continental Army has marched by following the bloody footprints in the snow.

Pretty much the only thing keeping the Americans alive is British general Howe's incompetence. Poor General Clinton begs permission to cross the Delaware River with six thousand soldiers to capture the rebel capital of Philadelphia and cut off Washington's retreat. But General Howe idiotically refuses, ordering Clinton hundreds of miles in the wrong direction to Newport, Rhode Island.

WORLDWIDE BRITISH MILITARY *vs.* AMERICAN MILITARY,

December 1776

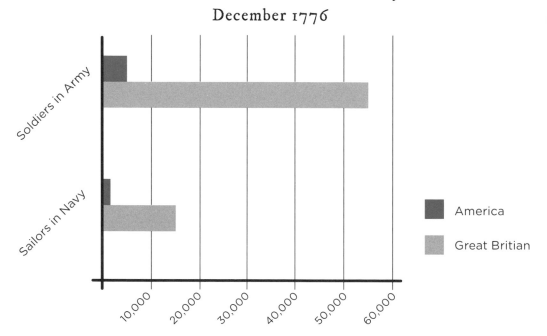

The Crisis

The Continental Congress has no money to pay for the rebel army. America is not yet a real country, so there is no US currency or taxes. The colonies are going into debt trying to pay for the army's clothing, food, and salaries. Worst of all for General Washington, nobody in America seems to have any gunpowder.

Washington has a measly three thousand troops left. His soldiers only signed up for one year's service, so the Continental Army is about a week away from disappearing completely. On the morning of December 19, Washington musters the last of his starving, shivering troops. Stand at attention by the Delaware

River and watch as Washington, his breath fogging in the cold, reads aloud to the soldiers a now famous pamphlet, *The Crisis*, written by a rebel patriot named Thomas Paine. . . .

"These are the times that try men's souls!"

The exhausted soldiers listen . . . and Washington winds up and delivers this gem for the history books:

"Tyranny, like hell, is not easily conquered; yet we have this consolation with us, that the harder the conflict, the more glorious the triumph."

The troops understand his message: the harder the fight, the sweeter the victory.

Because many of the soldiers are needed to guard supplies, ferries, and the wounded, Washington's effective fighting force is just 2,400 men. It will have to do. Washington has one week left to attack the British before his army disbands. He's spent most of 1776 retreating. Now, with his men starving and sick, he has no choice but to finally attack. Any victory at all will prove to his exhausted troops that they have a chance of winning. Washington sets his sights on the Hessian encampment in Trenton, New Jersey. The Hessian soldiers have food, shelter, warm clothes, and ammunition. If the American soldiers want those things, they must beat the Hessians.

Crossing the Delaware

Dress warmly on Christmas night. The weather will turn from rain to sleet to snow. You will march miles through the gale-force winds with no sleep. But tomorrow's battle will determine the course of the war and the future of America.

Washington issues each soldier sixty rounds of ammunition and three days of food rations. Men without boots tie rags around their feet. If you pass rebel lookouts in the darkness of night, the password is "Victory or Death."

Washington divides his army into three companies to attack Trenton from all sides. But two of the companies are unable to cross the frozen Delaware River. Washington has not even arrived

at Trenton, and already his army has shrunk to a thousand soldiers.

It is Henry Knox who is in charge of ferrying Washington's company of men across the Delaware River. After schlepping cannons from Fort Ticonderoga, Knox is used to dangerous river crossings. It's freezing in the storm, and chunks of ice threaten to destroy the transport boats. But somehow, Knox manages to get every soldier, horse, and cannon across without a single loss.

You and Washington's remaining soldiers must now march nine more miles through the blizzard before reaching Trenton. Men freeze to death on the night march—they pause for a rest and never get up again. Keep moving if you want to stay alive. Also: Merry Christmas.

BATTLE *of* TRENTON

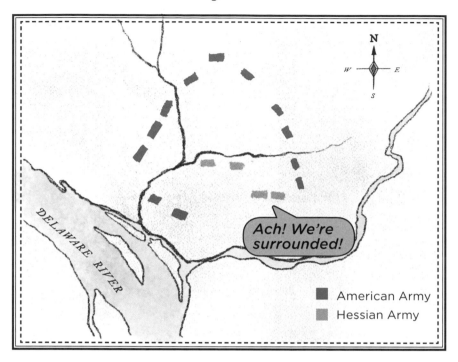

The Battle of Trenton

George Washington leads the attack on Trenton at eight in the morning on December 26, 1776. He races ahead of his troops, galloping into the fortified town. After months of defeats, the Continental Army finally begins working together like a well-oiled machine. When the American soldiers charge, each man tries to outrun his neighbor.

Henry Knox's artillery batters the Hessians. Twenty-one-year-old Alexander Hamilton is deathly ill, but rouses the strength to fight anyway. He commands the cannon crews that secure the heart of the town.

The Hessians are shocked to discover Americans attacking the day after Christmas, and after such a fierce storm. Caught completely off guard, the Hessians frantically move guns into position to fire grapeshot into the American troops. Grapeshot is seriously bad news. It's like filling a cannon with bullets. When the cannon fires, it sprays the bullets everywhere and can kill a dozen men with one blast.

Faced with certain death, General Washington's cousin, Captain William Washington, charges toward the Hessian cannons along with an eighteen-year-old lieutenant. Together, they slaughter the Hessian gun crews and turn the big guns on the rest of the Hessian army. Captain Washington's hands are badly wounded, and the young lieutenant is carried off the battlefield bleeding heavily with a musket ball in his shoulder. Don't worry—the boy will live. His name is James Monroe and he'll go on to become the fifth president of the United States.

★ BATTLE OF TRENTON SCOREBOARD ★

	British	Americans
Killed:	220	0
Wounded:	835	5
Captured:	1,000	0
Total Losses:	1,105	5

★ **Winner:** AMERICA

The Americans smash the Hessian mercenaries in an overwhelming victory. When the smoke clears, the Americans have only five wounded and no dead. George Washington proves the Continental Army can fight and win.

Impressed by this victory, France agrees to secretly lend much-needed money and aid to the new country. The king of France gets his relative, the king of Spain, to kick in some money as well. France and Spain were both utterly trounced by the British in the Seven Years' War. Sending aid to the Americans will help France and Spain stick it to their tea-drinking British enemies. So after a year of defeats, America will now begin to fight back.

TIME CORP! ™ SERVING YESTERDAY,
FOR A BETTER TOMORROW, TODAY. ™

LETTERS FROM TIME CORP'S COMPLAINT DEPARTMENT

Office of Jillian Mortimer
Assistant to the Second Assistant
of the Vice Assistant's Executive Assistant
Complaint Department

Valued Customer,

To file a complaint, you must fill out a complaint file. A complaint file to file a complaint will only be filed once a complaint file has been filed. You cannot file a complaint file unless you have filed a complaint file.

The truth is, we haven't replied to a complaint in seventeen years. At last count, there were 4.7 million outstanding complaints. We're not concerned about being seventeen years behind on responding to complaints, because, hey— time travel. We could decide to do them all in a century or two and be done with them by last week.

Occasionally, we like to post a few complaints in our guidebooks for our own amusement. Here are some of our faves:

"My family and I were enjoying our tyrannosaurus hunt on our Cretaceous safari, but got left behind when our Time Corp guide went home early to catch the Knicks game. Now we're stranded in a swamp being hunted by velociraptors. Can you please send help, or at least better Wi-Fi?"

—*The Clarksons. Mom, Dad, Sally, Bobby, and Junior*

"Some hooligan time traveler has stolen my stovepipe hat four score times this month. I'm trying to win a Civil War over here. The prankster keeps telling me he's selling my hats on something called 'the Internet.' I would either like him to stop, or I want a split of the profits."

—*Abraham Lincoln*

"I was flying across the Pacific on July 2, 1937, trying to set a world record, when some time-traveling jokester transported me to the Paleolithic Period. Now I'm stuck in a cave with a bunch of Neanderthals. This isn't funny!"

—*Amelia Earhart*

8

PAYBACK TIME

You're not out of the woods yet. General Washington has kicked
the hornet's nest. The British are not thrilled about the Hessian
defeat at Trenton. British general Cornwallis gathers eight thousand redcoats to attack the Continental Army in New Jersey.

Remember, Washington has an even bigger problem. On the
evening of December 31, most of his army's enlistments are ex-
piring. He hopes that the victory at Trenton will inspire his men
to stay. You can watch as he rides his white horse in front of the
troops and asks them to fight one more month, saying:

> *"My brave fellows, you have done all I asked you to do, and
> more than could be reasonably expected; but your country is at
> stake, your wives, your houses and all that you hold dear. . . . If
> you will consent to stay only one month longer, you will render
> that service to the cause of liberty and to your country which
> you probably never can do under any other circumstances."*

At first, no soldier volunteers to reenlist. Finally, a single soldier steps forward. Then a second, and a third, until finally, nearly all the soldiers choose to keep fighting.

People to Have Lunch With:
BETSY ROSS

In 1777, Congress adopts the "stars and stripes" to be the official American flag. Betsy Ross is believed to have sewn the first American flag when she was twenty-four years old. Stop by her house in the spring of 1776 when General George Washington pops over to discuss plans for the flag. He sketches her a design with thirteen stars and stripes to symbolize the thirteen colonies.

General Washington favors six-pointed stars, which

have a more biblical look. But Betsy Ross shows him on the spot how it's much easier to cut five-pointed stars out of cloth. Washington gives it the thumbs-up, and Betsy Ross's star is born.

Betsy herself was born on January 1, 1752, the eighth of seventeen children. *Seventeen children*— think about that. That's an entire classroom. How did her parents remember all of their kids' names? How did they all fit around a breakfast table? How did her family even afford so many breakfasts? And where did everyone sleep? Eight of Betsy's brothers and sisters died in childhood, but still, that leaves nine kids at the breakfast table. Nine! That's enough people for Betsy's family to form their own soccer team.

Betsy marries John Ross when she is twenty-two.[*] He serves as a member of the Pennsylvania militia and is killed in a gunpowder explosion. Even so, Betsy helps the Continental Army throughout the Revolutionary War, repairing uniforms, sewing tents, making blankets, and packing paper cartridges with musket balls. She even claims to do some tailoring for George Washington.

---

[*] Interestingly, Betsy's wedding certificate was signed by the governor of New Jersey, William Franklin . . . Benjamin Franklin's son. You may remember that Benjamin Franklin was also born into a family with seventeen children. We're not sure what these strange coincidences mean, but Finn Greenquill is convinced they add up to something.

Life in the Continental Army

You've probably figured out by now that life in the Continental Army isn't exactly easy. By July 1777, soldiers are paid less than seven dollars a month and the rate of desertion is close to 25 percent. The Continental Army starts paying soldiers to join. So soldiers join, desert, and join again under a new name—it's a great way to make easy money.

DAILY RATIONS FOR A CONTINENTAL SOLDIER

- 1½ pounds of flour or bread
- 1 pound of beef or fish or ¾ pound of pork
- 1 gill of whiskey*

If this doesn't sound good enough for you, and you're considering deserting to the British Army, keep in mind that the British soldiers aren't fed *that* much better.

DAILY RATIONS FOR A BRITISH SOLDIER

- 1½ pounds of flour or bread
- 1 pound of beef or ½ pound of pork
- ¼ pint of canned peas or 1 ounce of rice
- 1 ounce of butter
- 1½ gills of rum

---

* A gill is about a half cup.

Still, being a soldier isn't nearly as bad as being a Time Corp travel writer.

DAILY RATIONS FOR A TIME CORP TRAVEL WRITER

- 1 bowl of lumpy nutrition porridge
- 1 glass of green vitamin serum
- 3-hour lecture from Finn Greenquill on the importance of time management
- 1-dollar bonus for overtime hours
- 2-dollar deduction for being slow enough to require overtime hours

HELPFUL HINTS:
WOMEN IN THE ARMY

While life in the army is rough, a lot of patriotic Americans believe in the cause of freedom and want to join the fight. But what do you do if you're a woman? Women aren't allowed to fight in the Continental Army. Well, you may want to do what Massachusetts patriot Deborah Sampson does—dress up like a man and serve anyway.

At age twenty-one, Deborah Sampson dons her disguise and enlists in the Massachusetts Light Infantry under the name Robert Shurtleff. Deborah is one of many women who manage to sneak into the Continental Army, even while so many men are trying to sneak out.

In her first battle, outside Tarrytown, New York, Deborah is slashed across the forehead and hit with two musket balls in the thigh. She begs her fellow infantrymen to leave her to die because she does not want a doctor to discover her secret. The soldiers in her regiment, refusing to abandon her, fetch a horse and ferry her to a hospital. A doctor treats her head wound, but Deborah steals out of the hospital before he can cut away her pants to treat the musket wounds.

You may think you've had some bad days in your life, but odds are you've never had to sneak out of an army hospital with two bullets in your leg. Deborah performs surgery on herself, removing one of the musket balls with a penknife and a sewing needle. The other musket ball is too deep to reach, so she just leaves it in there. Though Deborah's leg never fully heals, she continues to serve until the end of the war.

After the Revolution, Deborah falls on hard times. Her friend Paul Revere lobbies Congress to pay her a full military pension, even though she is a woman. After many years, Congress finally agrees. Deborah goes on to marry and have three children. She dies of yellow fever at age sixty-six.

HELPFUL HINTS:
PUNISHMENT IN THE CONTINENTAL ARMY

If you are caught stealing livestock, you may receive one hundred lashes. If you really misbehave, you may receive up to one thousand lashes (which will probably kill you). If you desert the army, you may be sentenced to death.

If you are sentenced to a lashing, you'll be tied to a tree or post, your shirt will be stripped off, and you'll be whipped with a knotted cord. Each strike may break the flesh. One trick for dealing with the pain is to clamp a lead musket ball between your teeth to bite down on. Soldiers will often chew right through a musket ball during a lashing. It's the job of the drummers to administer the lashing, so make sure you're nice to them.

If you aren't sentenced to a lashing, here are some other common punishments:

- A log is chained to your leg.
- You are confined to bread and water.
- You are whipped with a birch rod.
- You are "picketed." This means you're suspended by the wrists from a rope with a sharp stake under your feet. Either your wrists or your feet are going to hurt. It's your choice!

The Battles of Saratoga

The Continental Army is on a roll. Washington wins an important victory over the British at Princeton, New Jersey. This is followed by an even bigger victory in New York.

British general John Burgoyne marches an army of over seven thousand soldiers down from Canada and runs into some serious, serious problems. His plan is to join forces with General William Howe in New York. But William Howe—who is so bad for the British that he might as well be working for the Americans—changes plans. Howe marches to Philadelphia, stranding Burgoyne in northern New York.

Burgoyne, abandoned deep in American territory, is in hot water. His supplies and communications are cut off. The Continental Army closes in like a pack of wolves. American militiamen converge on Burgoyne, attacking from all sides. Burgoyne's men are strung out in a long line along the forest trail and make for easy pickings. The Americans, led by General Horatio Gates and Major General Benedict Arnold, kill 440 British and wound 695. Burgoyne surrenders his entire army to the Americans—6,222 men. As usual, way to go, William Howe.

★ BATTLE OF SARATOGA SCOREBOARD ★

	British	Americans
Killed:	440	90
Wounded:	695	240
Captured:	6,222	0
Total Losses:	7,357	330

★ **Winner:** AMERICA

The British Take Philadelphia

Well, the good times can't last forever. In September 1777, General Howe successfully attacks the American capital—Philadelphia. We have to hand it to him—Howe earns this victory. General Washington makes some legitimate mistakes (including using inaccurate maps of the battlefield). But the British are simply more experienced and better organized. The American Continental Congress flees from Philadelphia to Lancaster, Pennsylvania. Washington's army retreats twenty miles to winter in Valley Forge. Times are about to get very, very tough for the Americans.

The Winter at Valley Forge

On December 19, 1777, Washington's hungry and tired army limps into Valley Forge. Four thousand of the army's twelve thousand soldiers are so poorly clothed, they are declared unfit for duty. Fully one-third of the men do not even have shoes. Without proper food or shelter, the men begin freezing to death. Over this lovely winter, 2,500 soldiers and 700 horses die of starvation or disease. Somehow, Washington's army is even worse off than it was a year ago.

The generals' wives, including Martha Washington, Kitty Greene, and Lucy Knox, help throughout the winter—cooking food, mending uniforms, and tending the sick—but soldiers continue to die and desert. There aren't enough axes to build huts, and logs have to be schlepped from miles away. Washington orders soldiers to include windows in their huts, because the airless cabins make diseases fester. For your next time travel vacation, you may want to choose the Mayan Empire in Central America—the weather is much more pleasant.

⭐☆☆☆☆

> **Food:** ★
> **Noise Level:** Eerily quiet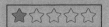
> **Décor:** ★
> **Outdoor Seating:** Yes ✔
> **Service:** ★
> **Accepts Credit Cards:** No ✖
> **Cost:** Free
> **Attire:** Rags
> **Wi-Fi:** No
> **Parking:** None. Hungry
> soldiers will eat your horse.

Valley Forge may not be the most pleasant vacation of your life. Rumors abound of starving soldiers eating bark off the trees or boiling grass stew. Most men live off "firecake"—flour and water baked in a kettle. These flat, dense, flavorless "breads" are filled with little bugs like weevils and maggots. But if you have to choose between eating firecake and starving, you should choose the lesser of two weevils.*

Here are what some of our readers say about wintering at Valley Forge:

★★ "This was wonderful for my diet. I lost fifteen pounds!"
—Mark Klutzky, Tempe, AZ

★★★ "The food is a step up from the swill they serve in the Time Corp employee cafeteria."
—Sandra Peterson, former Time Corp employee

★ "For the love of God, please send us something to eat! Maybe a couple of sandwiches? Some tuna fish? Anything!"
—General George Washington

---

* Finn Greenquill made us include that line. We, the good writers of Time Corp, had absolutely no say in the matter.

How to Survive the Continental Army

Europe Gives a Helping Hand

Let's face it: Washington's army is extremely young and inexperienced. The average age of the generals at Valley Forge is only forty. The average age of the officers is twenty-eight. Officer James Monroe is twenty. Officers Alexander Hamilton and Aaron Burr are twenty-two.

Experienced European officers, who currently have no wars to fight in Europe, begin volunteering for free in Washington's army.* They have their reasons. For one, career soldiers need to fight in wars if they want to climb the job ladder and win glory. And many of these soldiers, ruled by kings in their own countries, believe in the Americans' battle for freedom. The French aristocrat the Marquis de Lafayette, for example, sails to America to join the rebels, serves at Valley Forge, and will fight heroically throughout the Revolution. Baron Friedrich von Steuben is a German drill sergeant who spends the winter of 1777 whipping Washington's untrained army into top military condition. With strong European leaders, the American army is learning to fight.

On February 6, 1778, the French sign an alliance with the United States. After learning of the massive victory over Burgoyne at Saratoga, the French decide the Americans actually have a chance of winning. This time, the French aren't just lending money. The French army and navy will join the Americans on the field of battle.

In the springtime, fish fill the Schuylkill River, providing the men with food. The soldiers are ordered into the river to take their first bath all year.† The snows melt, and food and supplies begin rolling into the camp. The Continental Army survives the winter.

....

* Finn Greenquill can't understand why anyone would do anything for free. But in the 1700s, many career soldiers live for the opportunity to gain honor on the battle-field and will fight for their beliefs rather than a paycheck.

† Knowing the past five thousand years of human civilization, it is safe to say that one of the greatest human inventions, hands down, is the shower. How did anyone in history ever feel like they'd even woken up in the morning? It's a miracle anyone in 1778 ever got out of bed. The most amazing thing about the Founding Fathers isn't that they fought a revolutionary war, wrote a constitution, and invented modern democracy; it's that they did it without first having a shower.   —Finn Greenquill

People to Have Lunch With:
ALEXANDER HAMILTON

ALEXANDER HAMILTON

Alexander Hamilton is just twenty-two years old during the winter at Valley Forge. He is born on the tiny island of Nevis in the British West Indies to a single mother and is raised in poverty. When his mother dies, Hamilton becomes an orphan and must go to work as an accounting clerk at age eleven. At this point, Time Corp estimates Hamilton's odds of becoming one of the most important Americans in history to be .0000000001 percent.

The thing is, Hamilton is brilliant. At age sixteen,

he publishes an essay in a local paper that is so well received, readers raise money to send him to Columbia University in New York for college. Now his odds of becoming one of the most important Americans in history are up to .00000003 percent.

When war breaks out with England, Hamilton joins the New York Provincial Artillery Company and fights bravely in the Battles of Brooklyn, White Plains, Trenton, and Princeton. By 1777, the twenty-two-year-old Hamilton has so impressed General Washington, he is promoted to lieutenant colonel and becomes the general's secretary—writing speeches and letters for the future president. Now his odds of becoming key to the future of America are up to 5 percent.

In 1788, Hamilton writes a series of essays convincing New Yorkers to agree to a framework of rules and ideas that will govern the new country. These ideas form the basis for the United States Constitution. When Washington is elected president of the United States in 1789, he appoints Hamilton as the first secretary of the treasury. Hamilton single-handedly figures out the modern financial system—creating a national bank, national bonds, and a system of tax collection. He also finds time to create the US Coast Guard and the *New York Post*. Odds of changing the course of American history? One hundred percent.

In 1804, Hamilton attends a dinner party and makes a few scandalous remarks about a fellow politician and war veteran named Aaron Burr. These remarks somehow make it into the local paper. Incensed, Burr challenges Hamilton to a pistol duel at dawn on July 11, 1804, in Weehawken, New Jersey.

Hamilton does not wish to harm Burr, but he cannot lose honor by refusing the duel. He doesn't want to be a murderer or a coward. So Hamilton chooses to fire his gun into the air. Aaron Burr, however, has no qualms about shooting Alexander Hamilton. The great statesman and Founding Father dies of his wounds the following day. He is forty-seven.

HELPFUL HINTS:
THOMAS JEFFERSON'S MOOSE

America may owe its French alliance to the fact that Thomas Jefferson ships a dead moose to Paris in 1778. Okay, this deserves some explanation. . . .

Benjamin Franklin, John Adams, and Thomas Jefferson all serve as ambassadors to France. Many of the French believe that America is all swampland, with only small animals, and that any human raised in America must be small and "inferior" as well. This theory of American "inferiority" may seem crazy now. But many French believe it in 1778 and are reluctant to support the American cause.

Thomas Jefferson points out to the French that he

was raised in America, and he is six foot two. But this does not change the mind of French scientists. Making a long story short, Thomas Jefferson decides that shipping a moose to France will prove that America has larger animals than any in Europe. So Jefferson convinces the governor of New Hampshire to shoot a moose. The moose is killed twenty miles from the nearest road and is dragged through the snow for fourteen days. By the time it arrives in France by ship, its fur is decayed and the antlers are missing. But the skeleton alone is enough to convince French naturalists of two things: (1) moose do exist, and (2) they are very big. While French scientists never recant their theory, the French diplomats do decide to offer the Americans their alliance.

9

THE BATTLE OF COWPENS

General Howe, after years of blundering, is finally forced to resign from the British Army. This is bad news for the Americans, because Howe is replaced by General Clinton, who is much, much smarter.

Okay, hold your nose and swallow the medicine: the next few years see a lot of British victories. But keep your chin up. This is *your* time travel vacation and you don't have to visit every humiliating defeat. Sure, the British wipe the floor with the southern colonies in 1779. And yeah, the British trap a healthy chunk of the American army in Charleston and utterly destroy them in 1780. And, okay, fine, American general Benedict Arnold turns traitor, joins the British, and leads a rampaging army of redcoats across the south, destroying supply houses, leveling foundries, and burning down mills. But you can skip all this. Let's face it, Time Corp doesn't make money by selling tickets to losing battles.

Let's time jump to a major turning point of the war: the Battle of Cowpens in South Carolina.* It is known as one of the greatest tactical victories in military history. By this point in the war, the most important conflicts are being fought in the south. The American rebels have lost a lot of battles, but they've learned a lot of lessons. They're slowly building a great navy and a powerful army. Saddle up your horse, and for this battle, you'll want to bring along your rifle. . . .

People to Have Lunch With:
JOHN PAUL JONES

John Paul, the father of the American navy, is born in Scotland in 1747. He starts his career on the sea at age

---

* Cowpens is the actual name of a town in South Carolina. Other names that were considered: Horsecages, Sheephuts, Goatcoops, Chickenbarns, and Duckshacks.

thirteen and works his way up to first mate by sailing on British merchant and slave ships in his teens. At age twenty-one, he is promoted to the top position when his own captain dies of yellow fever. He enjoys a successful career captaining British ships until he kills a mutinying sailor in a sword fight. The dead sailor has political connections, so John is forced to flee to America. He adds the last name Jones to hide from British authorities.

Joining the Continental Navy in 1775, John Paul Jones is extremely successful in capturing British merchant ships, bringing much-needed supplies and weapons to the American cause. The British consider Jones a pirate. The Royal Navy eventually loses 3,386 ships to rebel sailors like Jones during the Revolution.

In one daring raid on England, John Paul Jones's crew attempts to burn all two hundred ships in the British port of Whitehaven. Jones's crew first raids a local tavern to find lantern oil to set the fires. Once in the tavern, the sailors are unable to resist the urge to stop for a drink. One drink leads to two. Their raid loses the element of surprise, the British are notified, and Jones's crew barely escapes England with their lives.

On September 23, 1779, John Paul Jones's American ship takes on a British Royal Navy warship for the first time in history. This battle takes place off the northeastern coast of England, near Yorkshire. The British warship is huge, with two decks firing a total of forty-four cannons. Outgunned, Jones's crew uses ropes to grapple the two ships together so they can board. This is a knock-down, drag-out fight, with both ships blasting cannon broadsides at point-blank range. Wear your life preserver and a Time Corp™ bulletproof vest if you've got one. When the British captain calls on Jones to surrender, Jones replies, "I HAVE NOT YET BEGUN TO FIGHT!"

Jones himself aims and fires the cannon that knocks down the British mainmast. An American sailor, William Hamilton, climbs a sail, inches to the end of the yardarm, and hurls a grenade down into an enemy hatch. The grenade explodes, detonating the British gunpowder and blasting a hole in their ship. The British finally lower their flag in surrender. John Paul Jones's crew has time to evacuate before their own ship sinks. They've won the battle. And the world now knows there's a new player in town: the US Navy.

Daniel Morgan

When you arrive at the Battle of Cowpens in 1781, introduce yourself to Daniel Morgan—he will be the hero of the fight. When he was a teenager, Morgan and his cousin Daniel Boone drove wagons for the British during the French and Indian War. Morgan punched a British officer in an argument and received a punishment of 499 lashes—enough to kill a man. But Daniel

Morgan survived, and he spends the rest of his life hating the British Army.

When the Revolutionary War breaks out in 1775, Morgan immediately forms a squadron of deadly riflemen. Rifles are lightweight and accurate, and Morgan's team wreaks havoc on the British. They use guerrilla tactics, shooting the American Indian guides who lead the British through the wilderness before targeting the British officers.

"The Butcher"

On January 17, 1781, British Colonel Banastre Tarleton chases Morgan's soldiers across Cherokee County, South Carolina. Americans call Colonel Tarleton "The Butcher" for his alleged massacre of surrendered rebel soldiers at the Battle of Waxhaws. Tarleton's redcoats have only slept four hours in the past two days, but Tarleton is eager to fight Morgan's battalion. The Americans under Morgan's command are mostly untrained militia, and Tarleton smells an easy victory.

Trapped by the Broad River near the town of Cowpens, Morgan decides to stand and fight. He places his men on a hill in three rows: sharpshooters, untrained militia, and well-trained Continental troops. William Washington—George Washington's cousin—hides his cavalry behind the hill.

The weak militia hide the well-trained Continental troops

BATTLE *of* COWPENS SET UP

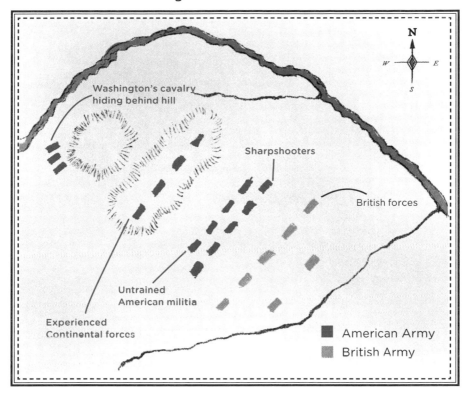

from the British. When Tarleton arrives, he sees only an untrained rabble—a tempting target. Morgan wants Tarleton to attack without thinking, and Tarleton takes the bait.

The exhausted redcoats charge uphill. Morgan instructs the untrained militia to fire two volleys—an achievable goal. The militia then fakes a panicked retreat behind the hill.

The British, excited to see the militia retreating, continue to attack uphill. They're shocked to find well-trained Continental soldiers waiting for them.

Now Morgan delivers his coup de grâce. The untrained militia runs all the way around the hill to attack the left side of the British Army. Washington's cavalry attacks the British's right. The British are stunned to find themselves in the middle of a rebel sandwich. Some exhausted redcoats are so astonished, they simply sit down on the battlefield in shock.

BATTLE *of* COWPENS MANEUVERS

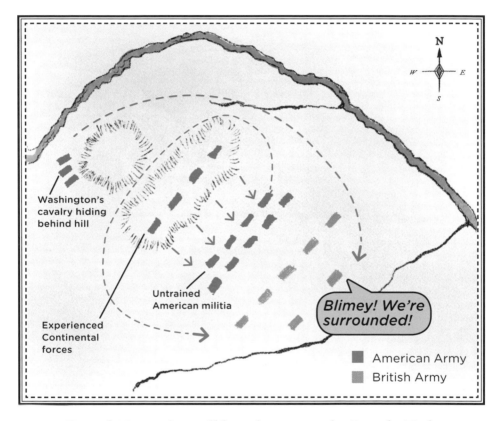

Daniel Morgan's small battalion routs the British. Tarleton escapes, but his brigade is wiped out of existence. The battle proves that the Americans are developing a world-class army and have a chance of winning the war, and winning their independence.

★ BATTLE OF COWPENS SCOREBOARD ★

	British	Americans
Killed:	110	25
Wounded:	229	124
Prisoners:	829	0
Total Losses:	1,168	149

★ **Winner:** AMERICA

NANCY HART

Here's an interesting meal to attend, if you don't mind the possibility of getting shot: Daniel Morgan's cousin Nancy Hart kills a troop of British soldiers over dinner.

Nancy Hart lives in the Georgia backcountry. She is tall and gangly, with red hair and a vicious temper. She's also known as a good hunter and an excellent shot.

One night, six British soldiers search her cabin,

looking for a rebel leader. Nancy tells them she hasn't seen the man.

Angry, one of the British soldiers shoots Nancy's best turkey and orders her to cook it up for dinner. The soldiers enter her log cabin, stack their weapons by the door, and start drinking Nancy's wine. As the soldiers drink, Nancy secretly sends her daughter to alert the neighbors.

Nancy then begins slipping the soldiers' muskets through an opening in the cabin wall. When the soldiers look up from their wine and realize what's happening, Nancy grabs a gun and fires a warning shot, saying she'll shoot the next man who moves.

A man moves.

Nancy shoots him. She holds off the rest of the soldiers until her husband, Benjamin, arrives. Together, they hang all six soldiers and bury them in the backyard.

10

VICTORY

If you're still alive, give yourself a pat on the back. You survived the massive naval assault at the Battle of Brooklyn, you didn't freeze to death while crossing the Delaware River on Christmas of 1776, and you staved off starvation in the winter at Valley Forge. Now it's time to bring the war to the British.

The Siege of Yorktown

By 1781, the Spanish have also joined the American cause. Like the French, the Spanish fought against the British in the Seven Years' War, so they still want to beat the British now. When British general Cornwallis holes up in Yorktown, Virginia, with nine thousand British and Hessian troops, the Spanish Navy cuts off Cornwallis's supplies. The French Navy, also fighting alongside the Americans, arrives to bombard the British. And the Marquis de Lafayette's French troops join Washington's American troops to surround Yorktown.

SIEGE *of* YORKTOWN

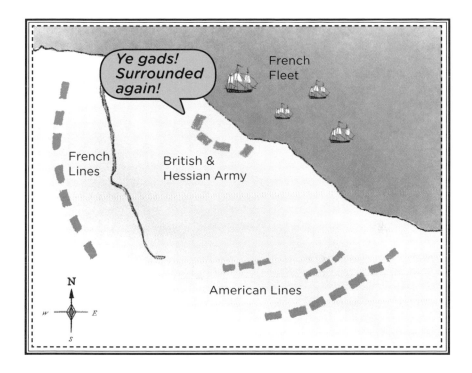

General Cornwallis knows he's toast. In an early example of germ warfare, he grows so desperate, he forces African Americans infected with smallpox to wander toward enemy lines in hopes of spreading the disease amongst the American troops.

By October 1, the trapped British are so hungry, they are slaughtering hundreds of their own horses for food. The French and American troops encircling the town are digging trenches to inch their cannons closer to the town walls. Soon, all the allied guns are in place. If you set your Time Corp Time Machine Colonial™ to 5:00 p.m. on October 9, you can watch General

Knox give George Washington the honor of firing the first cannon. Washington orders the bombardment to last all night so the British cannot make repairs to their shattered walls.

In the morning, Cornwallis orders his navy to sink more than a dozen of their own ships in the harbor to prevent them from being captured by the Americans. Cornwallis's only hope is to be rescued by fresh troops led by General Clinton. But Clinton's relief force does not arrive in time.

On the moonless night of October 14, Washington grants Alexander Hamilton's request to lead four hundred of the fastest American troops to attack the British wall. Hamilton's men race across a quarter mile of shell-strewn ground in ten minutes, then use axes to hack their way through the wooden spikes protecting the British earthworks. The Americans leap into a deep ditch dug by the British and stand on each other's shoulders to climb over the British wall. The whole time, the British are lobbing hand grenades down on the Americans. Hamilton's men, battling in the dark, are given strict instructions not to fire their muskets so they don't accidentally shoot each other; they fight only with bayonets (which the Continental Army finally has). Hamilton's assault is victorious, leaving only nine of his men dead and twenty-five wounded.

Hamilton's charge allows the French and Americans to place cannons even closer to Yorktown. With big guns bombarding Yorktown into smithereens, Cornwallis finally decides enough is enough. On the morning of October 17, 1781, a drummer appears on the British defenses, followed by an officer waving a white handkerchief in the universal sign of surrender. The Americans take nearly eight thousand prisoners, as well as 214 artillery pieces, several thousand muskets, twenty-four transport ships, the remaining British wagons, and the uneaten horses.

★ SIEGE OF YORKTOWN SCOREBOARD ★

	British	Americans
Killed:	309	88
Wounded:	595	301
Captured:	7,685	0
Total Losses:	8,589	389

★ **Winner:** AMERICA

People to Have Lunch With:

JAMES ARMISTEAD LAFAYETTE

James Armistead is an African American slave who serves the Continental Army as a double agent. His spying helps the Americans defeat the British at the Siege of Yorktown.

With his master's permission, James Armistead volunteers to join the Continental Army in 1781. The Marquis de Lafayette, the French officer and friend of General Washington's, sees Armistead's potential and employs him as an American spy. Armistead poses as a runaway slave and enters Benedict Arnold's camp (you remember Benedict Arnold—the American traitor who is now a British general). Armistead gains Benedict's trust, serving as a local guide, and soon pretends to spy for the British. As a double agent, he feeds the British false information while sending good information to the Americans.

After Benedict Arnold is redeployed in the north, Armistead enters General Cornwallis's camp and repeats his runaway slave act. British officers speak openly in front of Armistead, never suspecting a slave can be a spy. Armistead records information on British troop deployments and supplies, and slips these documents to other American spies to deliver to General Lafayette.

After the Revolution, James Armistead's master, William Armistead, tries to grant James his freedom, but is denied by Virginia law. After appeals from William Armistead and the Marquis de Lafayette, the Virginia legislature finally grants James his freedom in 1787. James changes his name to James Armistead Lafayette, to honor his general. As a free man, Armistead becomes wealthy and eventually buys three slaves of his own.

Forty-one years after the war, President James Monroe invites the Marquis de Lafayette to return to the United States. Lafayette travels to Virginia to visit George Washington's grave. A large crowd shows up to cheer the French war hero. When Lafayette spots his old friend James Armistead in the crowd, he orders his carriage to halt. Lafayette springs from his carriage, and the two old men embrace.

Peace

The Siege of Yorktown is the last major battle of the American Revolution. Britain is losing too much money fighting a long and costly war. The British government isn't thrilled that Spain and France have joined the American cause, and doesn't fancy the idea of fighting a world war. Benjamin Franklin—who is not only America's greatest writer and inventor, but is also America's greatest ambassador—works out a peace treaty with England.

After years of war, George Washington longs to return home to his farm in Mount Vernon and enjoy a peaceful retirement. Instead, he's elected to be the first president of the United States. It's yet another job he doesn't want and didn't ask for. Reluctantly, he packs his bags and leaves Mount Vernon once again.

The United States of America

The Founding Fathers bang out a constitution in 1787,[*] laying the groundwork for American democracy. It's not a perfect system because it includes jury duty. But all things being equal, it beats being ruled by a clinically insane monarch.

The beauty of the Constitution is that it lays out the basic rules for the world's first democracy since ancient Rome.[†] The original thirteen colonies become states in a single union, joined together by common cause. Suddenly, citizens have the right to vote for all their leaders. The Constitution also includes a Bill of Rights, guaranteeing freedoms found nowhere else in the world—freedom of speech, freedom of press, freedom of religion, and the right to a fair and speedy trial. The Americans are given the right to criticize their own government, and they've never stopped since.

The Revolution is won. Americans in 1788 have the most freedom and democracy of any country in world history.[‡] And

....

[*] Ben Franklin is involved with writing the four most important documents of the American Revolution: the Declaration of Independence, the US Constitution, the alliance with France, and the peace treaty with the British. Next to Ben Franklin, everyone else in the world is just plain lazy.

[†] If you haven't read *The Thrifty Guide to Ancient Rome*, Finn Greenquill would like to point out that it is fabulously entertaining and worth every penny. It will change your life, make you a better person, and possibly even improve your golf swing.

[‡] Okay, granted, if you are a woman or slave in 1788, you don't have much in the way of freedom or democracy. In fact, you really have none of either. But America is a work in progress, and the Revolution will prove to be a pretty decent step in the right direction for human rights the world over.

perhaps best of all, they can finally start drinking tea again.

Bright and hardworking people from around the world begin immigrating to America to enjoy the newfound rights and freedoms guaranteed by the Constitution. The country grows, and soon new states are formed and added to the union. America becomes a hotbed of ideas and innovation. Over the years, Britain, France, Spain, and many other countries will become more democratic, as well—inspired by the example set by America.

Meanwhile, America enjoys a profitable peace with England . . . at least until 1812, when the British come over and burn down the White House. But that is a story for another Time Corp time travel vacation.

A FRIENDLY MESSAGE FROM YOUR CORPORATE OVERLORD AT TIME CORP

Finn Greenquill here, CEO of Time Corp. I hope you've enjoyed reading this time travel guide as much as I've enjoyed playing moon golf while my writers hammered this thing out.

I'll admit, I haven't actually read this book. It's over a hundred pages. I mean, what kind of a hoser has time to read this? I've got a mega-corporation to run, and a mega-yacht that won't race itself!

Okay, okay, my publicist says I should apologize to all the hosers out there for that last paragraph, in which I called you all hosers. You are all valuable customers. And without hosers like you paying for overpriced time travel vacations to incredibly dangerous moments in history, I wouldn't be the lovable quadrillionaire that I am today.

Okay, scratch that last paragraph, too. Diplomacy is not my strong suit. My strong suit is made of bulletproof titanium and is currently being fitted with laser cannons. What was I talking about?

Ah, yes. Thank you to all the hosers. And to all the Time Corp travel writers who sacrificed their family time, their health benefits, and the majority of their limbs, I would like to sincerely and humbly say, get back to work.

Sincerely,

Finn Greenquill

Finn Greenquill
Corporate Overlord, Time Corp

SELECTED BIBLIOGRAPHY

Chernow, Ron. *Alexander Hamilton*. New York: The Penguin Press, 2004.

Franklin, Benjamin. *The Autobiography of Benjamin Franklin*. Edited by Charles W. Eliot LLD. USA: Tribeca Books, 2007.

McCullough, David. *1776*. New York: Simon & Schuster, 2005.

Philbrick, Nathaniel. *Bunker Hill: A City, a Siege, a Revolution*. New York: Penguin Books, 2014.

Vowell, Sarah. *Lafayette in the Somewhat United States*. New York: Riverhead Books, 2015.

ACKNOWLEDGMENTS

The travel writers at Time Corp would like to thank Finn Green-quill for his phenomenal talent, his effervescent wit, and his willingness to consider giving us one day of paid holiday next year.

A special thanks to the brilliant Leila Sales, who works for Penguin, but is not an actual penguin. A grateful tip of the hat to fact-checker Peter Walker, who was foresighted enough to delete the chapter on the Great Pancake Eating Contest of 1777, held between George Washington, William Howe, Finn Greenquill, and a dancing bear. A fond thank-you to copyeditors Laura Stiers, Krista Ahlberg, and Roman goddess of research Janet Pascal for catching all the misteaks in this book. A hearty clap on the back to art director Jim Hoover for vacuuming up the messy text and replacing it with graceful design. And a big high-five to design assistant Mariam Quraishi, for making Jim look good.

And finally, a gigantic thank-you to fellow time travelers Zach Greenberger and Brianne Johnson.

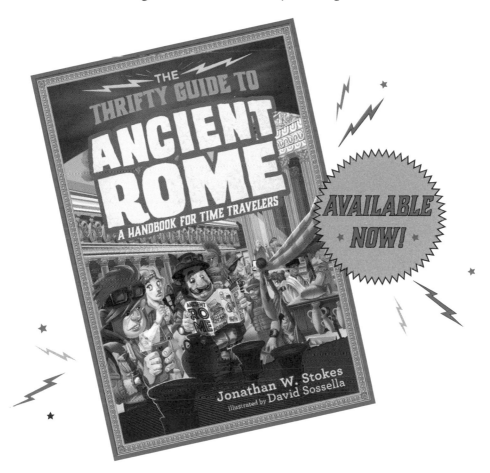